SUSSEX
STEAM

SUSSEX STEAM

MICHAEL HYMANS

AMBERLEY

First published 2016

Amberley Publishing
The Hill, Stroud
Gloucestershire, GL5 4EP

www.amberley-books.com

British Library Cataloguing in Publication Data.
A catalogue record for this book is available from the British Library.

ISBN 978 1 4456 6306 7 (print)
ISBN 978 1 4456 6307 4 (ebook)

Typeset in 10pt on 13pt Sabon.
Typesetting and Origination by Amberley Publishing.
Printed in the UK.

Contents

Preface

Sussex is not the most industrialised county in the country and, unlike others, was not renowned for its double-headed steam engines hauling long, snaking lines of coal wagons. Nevertheless, most of the stations, whether small or large, had their own goods yards offering a daily service, typically with an 0-6-0 in charge of the pick-up goods.

Electrification in the 1930s saw the end of many express steam services, but Newhaven Harbour boat trains remained steam-hauled, with Brighton Atlantics often in charge. Many branch lines were not electrified and steam was invariably used until Beeching's axe led to the demise not only of steam but of the branch itself.

Obviously most of the older engines illustrated started their working lives with the London, Brighton & South Coast Railway, but the formation of the Southern Railway saw classes from the neighbouring L&SWR and SE&CR running over Sussex metals, in addition to newer Southern engines designed by R. E. L. Maunsell and O. V. S. Bulleid. The formation of British Railways resulted in new standard designs of locomotives being seen around the county.

We were aware that many books have been published on the subject in the past; however, the majority of our archive of images has never been seen in print before. I wanted every photograph used in the book to be recognisable as being taken in Sussex, and it soon became evident that our collections could not satisfy this requirement; consequently, I have included photographs from other sources.

For this I am indebted to Edwin Wilmshurst, Ian D. Nolan, Paul Edwards of ASLEF, Ernie Brack, John Law, John Scrace, Keith Harwood , Worthing Library and Newhaven Local History Museum for letting me use photographs from their superb collections. I hope I have not breached anybody's copyright; apologies if I have. Please contact the publisher if this is the case.

The Main Line to Brighton

The main line to Brighton was built by the London & Brighton Railway, but used tracks owned by the London & Croydon Railway from London Bridge to Norwood. From there it joined forces with the South Eastern Railway to build tracks as far south as Redhill, where the two companies' lines diverged. After that point, the London & Brighton Railway was solely responsible for building the line to Brighton.

It was operated from 1846 by the London, Brighton & South Coast Railway (LB&SCR), which itself was an amalgamation of five companies: the London & Croydon Railway; the London & Brighton Railway; the Brighton & Chichester Railway; the Brighton, Lewes & Hastings Railway and the Croydon & Epsom Railway.

Just over the Sussex border at Gatwick Airport, but heading our way, was N class No. 31873, in charge of the 11.39 Eastbourne–Leicester service on 10 August 1963.

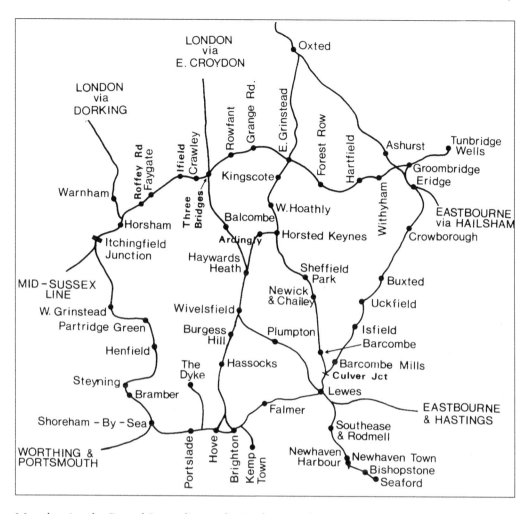

LONDON
via
E. CROYDON

LONDON
via
DORKING

Oxted

Rowfant

Grange Rd.

E. Grinstead

Forest Row

Hartfield

Ashurst

Tunbridge
Wells

Roffey Rd
Faygate

Ifield

Crawley

Three Bridges

Kingscote

Groombridge
Eridge

Warnham

Balcombe

W. Hoathly

Withyham

EASTBOURNE
via HAILSHAM

Horsham

Ardingly

Horsted Keynes

Crowborough

Itchingfield
Junction

Haywards
Heath

Sheffield
Park

Buxted

MID – SUSSEX
LINE

Newick
& Chailey

Uckfield

W. Grinstead

Wivelsfield

Partridge Green

Plumpton

Isfield

Henfield

Burgess
Hill

Barcombe

The
Dyke

Hassocks

Barcombe Mills

Steyning

Culver Jct

Bramber

Lewes

Shoreham – By – Sea

Falmer

EASTBOURNE
& HASTINGS

WORTHING &
PORTSMOUTH

Portslade

Hove

Brighton

Kemp Town

Southease
& Rodmell

Newhaven
Harbour

Newhaven Town

Bishopstone

Seaford

Map showing the Central Sussex lines radiating from Brighton.

The line crosses the Surrey/Sussex border between Horley and Gatwick. The first train to travel over these lines left London Bridge bound for Brighton on 21 September 1841. Only First Class passengers were allowed on this train or any other train travelling to Brighton, as the town did not want the working classes lowering the tone. Third Class passengers were soon catered for, however, as the railway company saw the potential of increased traffic. Fares were reduced to 3s 6d in 1843 with 360,000 passengers taking advantage of the lower fare in six months.

As the inaugural train travelled south through the county, the first station it passed through was Three Bridges. This is because a station at Gatwick was not opened until 1891, and even then this was only to serve the racecourse, only opening on race days. It was renamed Gatwick Racecourse in 1946, a name that it kept until 1958 when it became the Gatwick Airport station that we know today. The airfield was opened using part of the racecourse and gradually expanded until it had taken it over completely. In 1935 another station was opened just to the south of the present station called Tinsley

H Class 31005 and N Class 31832 await their next turns at Three Bridges shed in the summer of 1963.

A fine portrait of Class C2X No. 32535 on shed at Three Bridges on 11 June 1960. It was a 1908 Marsh rebuild of a R. J. Billinton design of 1900.

October 1963 saw a brace of Q1 0-6-0s on shed at Three Bridges, Nos 33017 and 33015; the steam crane is also busy. (Keith Harwood)

Green, but it was renamed Gatwick Airport within a year of opening. This station closed when the present Gatwick Airport station opened.

Three Bridges was originally going to be called 'Crawley', according to the plans drawn up by the architect, David Mocatta. Indeed, when it opened it was called Crawley. However, this was only until 1848 when the line to Horsham was opened; then it became Three Bridges, which was at that time a small village nearby. The locomotive shed opened in the same year. This was a two-road shed with a 45-foot turntable and water tank built on land between the main line and the proposed line to Horsham. It was later superseded by a larger three-road shed, a 60-foot turntable and a coaling stage. The shed was home mainly to tank engines and 0-6-0s used on local goods and passenger services.

Although the line from Redhill to Three Bridges is now quadruple, this was not the case at the time of the first train. It would take over sixty years before this came about. Since entering Sussex, the line had been fairly flat, with no large engineering works needed – but that was to change when it reached the Sussex Weald.

The first hurdle to overcome was Balcombe Tunnel. This is 1,141 yards long and took three years to build, being finished in 1841. Ingress of water from the hard sandstone above was not only a problem for the builders, but has remained a problem to this day. In the days of open carriages, passengers were protected from water falling onto them by galvanised metal sheets hung above their heads. These sheets proved to be a danger to passengers, however, as the increased air pressure caused by the trains was capable of ripping the sheets from their fixings. During the winter months, icicles would form,

Class D3 No. 32390 was in charge of an RCTS East Sussex railtour at Three Bridges on 4 October 1953.

LB&SCR Class D1 0-4-2T No. 258 of 1882 vintage at Three Bridges. The engine was named *Cosham* until 1906, when its nameplate was removed. It was withdrawn in 1926.

M7 No. 30029, bound for East Grinstead, waits to leave Three Bridges in the summer of 1963. (Keith Harwood)

Above: K class No. 32341 waits its next turn at Three Bridges shed on 5 August 1962. (Ernie's Railway Archive)

Right: Class H No. 31522 of 1904 vintage waits to leave Three Bridges from the East Grinstead/ Tunbridge Wells bay on 24 June 1962.

growing to such lengths that they became a danger to crews who had no cab roofs to protect them. The partial relining of the tunnel with engineering bricks between 1907 and 1909 was carried out in an attempt to alleviate the problem.

In 1881 a body was found inside the tunnel. Investigations showed that it was that of Frederick Gold, a retired businessman and coin dealer. He had been shot four times and stabbed by Arthur Lefroy Mapleton, who had stolen his watch and disposed of the body as they passed through Balcombe Tunnel. Mapleton was caught because a ticket collector opening the carriage door at Preston Park noticed that a passenger was bloodstained, and that his collar had been torn. The man claimed that he himself had been set upon by other passengers who had since fled. The railwayman's suspicions were aroused, however, when he saw a watch chain dangling from Mapleton's shoe. He was taken to Brighton police station, where he gave a statement saying he had been robbed. When the body was found, Mapleton became a suspect but, when police went to his house to arrest him, he had fled. A sketch of Mapleton was published by the *Daily Telegraph* and he was soon arrested at a guest house in Stepney. He was eventually found guilty of murder and hanged at Lewes prison.

This is not the only tragedy to befall the tunnel. During the First World War, three soldiers sheltered inside the tunnel from a passing Zeppelin airship but were killed by a passing train. A similar incident occurred during the Second World War, when two more soldiers sought shelter from an air raid but were also killed by a train. These incidents have led to tales of the tunnel being haunted.

No. 32528 was a Marsh rebuild of one of Billinton's B2 engines, designed for freight work in 1908. It is pictured at Haywards Heath shed on 25 September 1955. It was withdrawn in February 1961.

A second bore was planned in 1903 to allow the quadrupling of the tracks to continue further south but this never came about.

As late as 2011 the tunnel was still giving trouble. Catchment trays had been fitted beneath the ventilation shafts in 2006/7, and an inspection team noticed that some of the fixings had failed, leaving metal sheets hanging down just inches from the roofs of passing trains. The tunnel had to be shut, while additional support brackets were fitted.

As the line continued south, the next problem to be overcome was crossing the Ouse Valley. This was achieved by the construction of the magnificent Ouse Valley Viaduct. Designed by David Mocatta and engineered by John Rastrick, it took two years to build (1839–41) and is 1,475 feet long and 96 feet high. It has thirty-seven arches, which took over 11 million bricks to construct. The bricks were imported from Holland and reached the site by travelling up the River Ouse via Newhaven and Lewes. The track bed is lined by stone balustrades, with four square towers at either end. These were made with stone from Heddon Quarries near Newcastle. It cost £38,500 to build, which is about £3.5 million in today's money. These days the river below is hardly noticeable from the viaduct, being little more than a stream. The viaduct is now a Grade II* listed building and was restored in 1996 using stone imported from France to match the original.

Just south of the viaduct was to be a junction with the proposed Ouse Valley Railway. The LB&SCR had been given powers to build this line, which would have served Lindfield, Sheffield Park, Uckfield, East Hoathly, Chiddingly, Hailsham, Little Common, Bexhill and Bulverhythe before ending at St Leonards. This had not been proposed as a profitable venture, but as a way of deterring the London, Chatham & Dover Railway, as well as the South Eastern Railway, from making inroads into their territory by building lines to Eastbourne and Brighton. Work actually started on the line in 1866 and some embankments, cuttings and bridge abutments can still be seen. Work stopped in February 1867 due to the collapse of the Overend & Gurney bank, which was financing the construction.

Continuing the journey southwards, the next station reached was Haywards Heath. The LB&SCR operated a service as far south as here from 12 July 1841. Travellers wishing to reach Brighton had to switch to a stagecoach to continue their journey. The station buildings were again the work of David Mocatta.

Ouse Valley Viaduct with L&SWR T9 120 and Caledonian Single 123 heading south on an enthusiasts' special on 15 September 1963.

It was one of the first stations to be served by slip coaches. From 1858 coaches were slipped from Brighton expresses. These coaches then formed local trains towards Hastings. The system carried on until electrification in 1933. The station remained one of the busiest on the line, with the opening of the line towards Lewes at Keymer Junction, 3 miles to the south, and the opening in 1882 of the Lewes & East Grinstead Railway's line to Horsted Keynes via Ardingly from a bay at Haywards Heath station. This railway company merged with the LB&SCR on the opening of the line. Amazingly there wasn't a connection between the two lines until 1912, with the two lines running parallel until pointwork was installed, giving the company a secondary route to London.

This line was closed to passenger traffic in 1963 but, with the Bluebell Railway now having reached East Grinstead and having ambitions to reach Haywards Heath, this link may still be re-established one day. The line is still open as far as Ardingly for Hanson Aggregates freight trains.

Class T9 120 in L&SWR livery leaves Haywards Heath with a LCGB rail tour on 24 June 1962.

Class C2X No. 32536 being re-railed at Haywards Heath. (Charlie Verrall)

A Wainwright D class, No. 31734, introduced in 1901, nears Wivelsfield with the 09.25 Hastings–Wolverhampton service on 2 September 1955. (Charlie Verrall)

Another Wainwright class D, No. 31737, passes through Wivelsfield with the Up service to Birkenhead from Hastings on 19 May 1955. (Charlie Verrall)

In charge of a Stephenson Locomotive Society special was N15X No. 32329 *Stephenson*, passing Keymer Junction on 23 June 1956.

Immediately on leaving Haywards Heath there is another tunnel. This is relatively short, being only 247 yards long. It is also known as Folly Hill Tunnel. The first station to be encountered is Wivelsfield, which actually serves the town of Burgess Hill and is just north of Keymer Junction, where the line to Lewes and Eastbourne leaves the Brighton line. There used to be a station called Keymer Junction on the line to Eastbourne, but this closed in 1883 when plans were submitted to relay the junction.

When these plans were shelved, Parliament forced the company to build a new station north of the junction. The new Keymer Junction station was opened on 1 August 1886, but this name was changed to Wivelsfield in 1896. It was the site of a serious accident in December 1899, when a boat train from Newhaven collided with a train from Brighton, killing six passengers and injuring many more. The cause was thick fog obscuring the red signal. Improvements were made to the signals to make sure it did not happen again.

Leaving the station means that Brighton is just under 10 miles away but, with the South Downs in the way, the engineering on the line was not easy. Hassocks is the next station to be reached, although then it was called Hassocks Gate. It opened on the first day of the service and originally had four tracks – two with platforms and two for through trains. In the early 1880s, a new station building was erected and was the prototype for many such designs, including Sheffield Park on the Bluebell Railway. However, this was demolished in 1973. Soon after leaving Hassocks is Clayton Tunnel. It was the most challenging task to tunnel under Clayton Hill. It took 6,000 men three years (1838–41) to build the 1,730-yard-long tunnel. The northern end was another of Mocatta's masterpieces, with the portal constructed in the form of a castle. There is no definitive reason for why this

On 8 August 1958 an accident occurred at Hassocks involving Fairburn 2-6-4T No. 42086 and a 4SUB. It was caused because the Down-side ground frame was not interlocked with Hassocks signal box, and the engine started to leave the sidings into the path of the EMU.

was built, but theories include that the farmer whose land it was built on insisted on it or that it may have been to try to reassure passengers that travelling through the tunnel would be safe, as many thought that it would lead to certain death. A cottage was built between the turrets in 1849 to house the tunnel keeper, whose job it was to keep the gas lamps inside the tunnel alight. All tunnel linings were painted white to aid visibility and they were also lit by gas. The problem with this was that passing trains blew the gas lamps out and they constantly had to be relit.

In 1861 there was an accident inside the tunnel that claimed twenty-three lives and left over 150 injured. There was a signalling system in place that simply consisted of a man at each end of the tunnel. After a train had entered the tunnel, the signalman would return the signal to danger until the signalman at the other end had informed him by telegraph that it had left. On 25 August, three trains left Brighton heading for London in close succession. After the first one had entered the tunnel, the signalman was slow to return the signal to danger. As the second one approached, he waved a red flag but the train entered the tunnel. He then received a signal from the northern end that a train had left the tunnel, which he mistakenly took to be the second one, so he let the third one enter. Unfortunately the driver of the second train had seen the red flag being waved, stopped inside the tunnel and had started to reverse out again when the collision occurred. The majority of passengers killed were in the rear carriage of the second train when it was destroyed by the force of impact and scalding water from the engine. At the subsequent inquest both signalmen were found not to be blameworthy, but the assistant station master at Brighton was. This is because the rest of the line was signalled by time

The last of the Gladstones B172, nearing Hassocks with the 4.8 p.m. Brighton–London service. It lasted until September 1933, giving forty-two years of service.

frequencies with a gap of 5 minutes between trains. Charles Clegg, who was on duty that fateful day, was found guilty of manslaughter, having let all three trains depart with only 7 minutes separating them all. He was sent for trial but a jury found him not guilty.

Patcham Tunnel, which is 488 yards long, then has to be negotiated before the outskirts of Brighton are reached.

Just outside Brighton is Preston Park station. This was not open on the first day of the service, but the arrival of the railway in Brighton caused the town to expand rapidly. In fact it was the most rapidly expanding town in the country between 1841 and 1871. Preston had been a small parish when the railway arrived but, by 1869 when the station opened, it had been swallowed up by the incessant need for new housing. This area, however, was populated by those who were somewhat better off than those forced to live in rows of back-to-back terraced houses in the town centre and could afford a degree of segregation from the hordes of holidaymakers while still enjoying the benefits of living near the coast. The town had grown from 46,000 residents when the railway from London opened to just over 90,000 within thirty years. The station was originally just called Preston. Ten years later the station was enlarged to consist of two island platforms when a spur line was added, and it was then that it was renamed Preston Park. This spur line, known as the Cliftonville Curve, included a 535-yard tunnel and was built to serve Hove and stations to the west, negating the need to go into Brighton station and reverse. This shortened journey times and eased congestion at the terminus.

The first train took 2.5 hours to reach Brighton after leaving London. Although this is a long time by today's standards, it more than halved the journey time of the stagecoach. The line had cost over £2½ million to build.

It had not been everybody's choice of route either. Initially there was a choice of six routes, including one by Robert Stephenson, who favoured a longer but flatter route that went via Henfield and Horsham, with a terminus near Brunswick Square. This was favoured by some but definitely not by the influential residents of the square, who did not want a station anywhere near their houses. The government of the day were tiring of the arguments over which route should be built and regarded the building of the line as an important asset to the town; consequently they appointed their own engineer to report back. He published his report in June 1837, finding in favour of the shorter but more challenging route. John Rastrick was appointed chief engineer, a man with several years' experience, including being a judge at the Rainhill Trials. One of the reasons for deciding to site the station at its present location was that it would be easier to construct branches to Lewes in the east and Shoreham to the west than it would be if the station was built nearer sea level.

The first train to arrive from London was not the first train the town had seen, however. From the previous year, trains had been running westwards along the coast to Shoreham – but more of that later.

David Mocatta had been kept busy designing most of the company's major buildings; one of his finest was Brighton station, which was also the head office for the LB&SCR. It was built in the Italianate style, the frontage of which is now largely obscured by the awning over the taxi rank. The present wonderful station canopy was not built until 1882/3, and passengers arriving on the first train would have been sheltered from the elements by four separate canopies – one over the lines to Shoreham, with the other three covering the London tracks. These were 250 feet long, with their slate-covered roofs being supported by cast-iron columns. Brighton station was given Grade II* listed status on 30 April 1973.

The chosen site for the station was not the easiest to build on, as it was on a steep hillside 130 feet above sea level. The advantage of choosing this site was that it was high

Brighton station as built, before the awnings and the later train shed were added.

enough to build a viaduct for future lines to the east, as well as needing less groundwork for lines towards the west. Passengers leaving the station when it was built had to do so via Trafalgar Street, which is a steep hill to the left. It was so steep that horse-drawn vehicles could not make it up the hill, and so a cab road was built on the eastern side of the station buildings. Horse cabs arriving at the station turned right up this cab road, which ran between the station buildings and the goods shed. When the station was redeveloped in 1882, the cab road was altered as well. The gradient was reduced by introducing a hairpin, bringing the cab road out onto the platforms. When motor cars were introduced, they were unable to negotiate the sharp hairpin and the use of the cab road declined. The cab run was initially open air but when the station was extended and platforms built over the top, it was turned into a tunnel.

By this time Queens Road had been built, partly financed by the LB&SCR. From 1844 this gave passengers a much easier and grander route to the promenade. The cab road still exists but the entrance in Trafalgar Street is now behind two large locked wooden gates.

The goods yard, which was further down the hill, lay 30 feet beneath the level of the passenger tracks. Reaching it from the lines to the west proved to be a problem, as all the lines heading north had to be crossed to gain access to it. Initially a tunnel was built that ran diagonally beneath the platforms, but in 1852 a new line was laid, giving access to the yard from the London lines. The old tunnel still exists, but has been blocked up. During the Second World War, it was used to house offices and post-war the local rifle club was allowed to use part of it. Since then, the goods trains entering the yard from the west have had to reverse to gain access.

For Easter 1843, the directors decided to run an excursion train to Brighton from London. This was not to be an exclusively First Class train but was to include Second and Third Class carriages as well. Little could they have realised how popular it would be. Newspaper reports of the time printed stories of masses of people lining the route to watch the train pass. They were in for a long wait, however. It arrived one and a half hours late due to the number of passengers and the engines struggling to cope. Reports vary, with stories of needing three locos on the front and at times needing four engines banking the thirty-three coaches not uncommon. 1,000 people were estimated to have ridden on the train on the first day and 500 each on the next two days.

Excursion trains left for London as well, with about the same number of Brightonians heading towards the capital and taking advantage of the cheap fares on offer.

All of these visitors needed to be fed and entertained, too. Businesses sprang up offering food and drink, with many guest houses opening as well. By the 1860s there were more pubs in the town than grocers. On Monday mornings, more carriages had to be added to the London-bound trains to cater for those who had stayed for the weekend.

The more affluent residents who had been tempted to move to the town in the footsteps of the Prince Regent and had set up home in fine houses in streets like Royal Crescent were now having to share the town with more and more of the working classes. Streets and streets of back-to-back terraced houses had been built to cater for the increasing numbers employed by the railways in the workshops, as well as those on the operating side of the business.

Although the coming of the railway had undoubtedly brought expansion and prosperity to the town, the LB&SCR were not revered by all. The long, steep climb up to the station was proving to be too much for some, especially those who had moved to Brighton for health reasons. Owners of the better houses and hotels also complained about the distance of the station from their properties. Furthermore the poor complained that the fastest trains to London were for First Class passengers only, and those who could only afford 'Parliamentary' fares were subjected to longer, uncomfortable journeys. Commuters also complained about the siting of the London Bridge terminus south of the river, meaning a walk of 'the worst half-mile in London' to reach their places of work. Even the First Class passengers complained that there was no way to regulate the heating in their compartments. Poor souls!

In 1883 a Brighton direct scheme was put forward and won the approval of the local council. This railway would have a terminus adjacent to the Pavilion and leave in a westerly direction before heading north. It would tunnel under Queens Road, Dyke Road and Montpelier Road, emerging at Holland Park. From there it would serve Poynings, Bolney and Reigate before continuing through Sutton and Mitcham, joining LC&DR lines and terminating at Victoria.

Another scheme was put forward in 1901 by the London & Brighton Electric Railway. This company planned to build a new railway that was electrified all the way. The whole line was to be built between two unclimbable fences. It was claimed that the journey could be made in 30 minutes with fares reduced by over 50 per cent. Parliament threw this and other schemes out.

Many people travelled to Brighton on their way to the Continent via Dieppe. The steamers left from Shoreham, but called at the chain pier to pick up more passengers, which is where many passengers chose to board. This method of transport came to an end when the chain pier was washed away in a storm in 1896. By that time, the port at Newhaven had opened and passengers were taken straight to the dock instead of having to find the means of travelling between the station and the pier.

In June 1846 Brighton station was extended to include the tracks and platforms for the new route eastwards to be built by the Brighton, Lewes and Hastings Railway. This company had been bought by the London & Brighton in 1845, and so was absorbed into the LB&SCR in 1848. The BL&HR was formed to build a line eastwards, linking with the South Eastern Railway at Hastings, but the directors had been given parliamentary consent to sell it to the L&BR before it was even built.

The station was further extended during the mid/late nineteenth century, but its location limited this. In order to cater for more trains, the platforms were lengthened, allowing two trains to use one platform. This necessitated signals to be installed at the approach to the platforms, with not only a home but also a distant signal. If the distant signal was 'on', it meant there was already a train in the platform.

The small station canopies were replaced in 1883 by the grand, curved, double-apex structure that survives today. It was constructed over the top of the original canopies, which were removed on completion of the new one.

The 1883 alterations also included extending the station building eastwards. This entailed building a bridge over Trafalgar Street. A parcels depot was added and the front of Mocatta's building was masked by a new canopy, which gave shelter to passengers arriving by cab. A new clock with four faces was also installed; it is still suspended by Platform 7.

K class 2-6-0 No. 32346 simmers quietly at Brighton station. It was designed by L. B. Billinton and introduced in 1913.

Class E4 0-6-2T No. 32519 in one of the main-line platforms with a 6-PUL unit on the adjacent line.

A view from under the canopy, as an I3 4-4-2 tank leaves Platform 3 on 21 July 1951.

Until 1900 all trains to London had to go via Redhill, but when the Quarry Line was built between Earlswood and Coulsdon North, a faster route to London was created. Up until then the fastest journey between London and Brighton was timed at exactly one hour. This new line allowed a time saving of 5 minutes, and the fastest ever scheduled time was 55 minutes; however, as all trains now stop at East Croydon, this is now 58 minutes.

Electrification reached Brighton in 1933, which greatly decreased the number of steam locomotives needed, especially express passenger engines. Freight engines were still needed, in addition to tank engines, to operate the secondary branch lines through Steyning to Horsham, to Tunbridge Wells via Uckfield and to East Grinstead via Horsted Keynes.

Class D3 No. 32379 is seen leaving Brighton on a train to Horsham on 25 October 1952. The steep cliff sides on the right give an indication of how much chalk had to be removed to create a level surface on which to build the station.

Gladstone 0-4-2 B197 passes the works as it leaves Brighton with a six-wheeled coach ahead of a rake of bogie coaches. Originally named *Jonas Levy*, it was withdrawn in August 1932 after a life of forty-four years.

Brighton H2 Atlantic No. 32425 *Trevose Head* was in charge on this leg of the RCTS Brighton Works Centenary special on 19 October 1952.

Standard Class 4 No. 80015 leaves Brighton on 4 July 1953.

Schools Class No. 30906 *Sherborne* on 4 July 1953. The coach next to the engine is an ex-SECR birdcage brake with lavatories and a first-class coupe compartment. The other two are Maunsell Southern Railway side corridor coaches, built on SECR underframes. The train is leaving Brighton on a direct service to Hastings.

The West Coast Route

As stated earlier, the first train to leave Brighton was not bound for London, but Shoreham, 5.5 miles away to the west.

Why Shoreham? Well, it was to make use of the harbour facilities. With Brighton station being situated on a steep hillside, much material was needed to build up the terraces upon which it was constructed, as well as supplying the materials needed to construct the railway. A wharf was constructed on the western side of the harbour at Kingston.

Much material had to be taken away as well. On leaving Brighton, the line had to be cut through New England Hill. It took hundreds of workers to excavate the tons of chalk that had to be removed. They did have the help of two steam locomotives, though. These had been brought in by the London & Brighton Railway to transport rails and sleepers to the site. They were made by Jones, Turner and Evans at their Viaduct Foundry at Newton-le-Willows in 1839. One was a 2-2-2 numbered '1' and named *Brighton*, while the other was a 0-4-2 numbered '2' and named *Shoreham*. These engines were delivered by sea to Kingston and then dragged by teams of horses to the construction site.

Schools Class No. 30915 *Brighton* in Brighton station in 1959. (Ian D. Nolan)

Class B1 B618 at Brighton on 3 July 1926. (H. C. Casserley)

The first trains ran on 11 May 1840, before the station buildings and platforms had been finished. They were reserved for invited guests and took 11 minutes to reach their destination. They consisted of two Third Class, two Second Class and two First Class carriages, as well as three luggage vans. At precisely 3 p.m., to a fanfare from the band of the 12th Lancers, the train pulled out of Brighton, only to grind to a halt a few yards on. The reason for the delay was a brake that had locked on in one of the carriages. The company's engineer, Mr Rastrick, who was travelling on the train, alighted and managed to free the brake, and the train continued on its inaugural journey.

It was opened to the general public the following day when 1,750 passengers took advantage of the service. First Class passengers paid 1s; Second Class cost 9d; and Third Class 6d. Although the opening was a joyous event, within a week one young man had been killed. He had been sitting on the edge of a luggage wagon when the train jolted and he fell off, losing his life on the spot.

On weekdays a train left Brighton every two hours from 9 a.m. until 7 p.m., with the return journey every two hours from 10 a.m. Sundays saw five return journeys. Third Class travel was by open wagon, often with no seats, with the passengers not only open to the weather but also to the exhaust and smuts emitted from the engine. These trains were mixed, allowing the transfer of freight as well as passengers. New engines had been purchased to operate the service. These were 2-2-2 configurations: one named *Kingston* was built in 1839 by Sharp, Roberts & Co. of Manchester, and the other was named *Eagle* and built by G. & J. Rennie in 1840.

Marsh class I3 4-4-2T 21, introduced in 1907 at Brighton. It was withdrawn in September 1951.

Sidings at Hove were used to store locos that had been taken out of service and were awaiting a tow to the scrapyard. Here we see K class No. 32338. Other members of the class were all withdrawn at the end of 1962.

Another view of the scrap line at Hove with Nos 32338, 30923, 30911, 32417 and 32342 awaiting their end on 27 January 1963. (Ian D. Nolan)

E4 0-6-2T No. 32468 shunting 'The Lancing Belle' coaches at Hove as N 2-6-0 No. 31871 trundles past in October 1961. (Ian D. Nolan)

The first station on the line was Hove and it was built on the site of Holland Road goods yard. Class D3 0-4-4T No. 390 *St. Leonards* enters with a local stopping train.

In 1842, an engine called *Brighton* blew up as it was heading through Hove. The driver was severely scalded but the fireman escaped injury. Many parts of the engine, including the connecting rods, were blown some considerable distance.

In 1865 Hove station was opened, although at the time it was called Cliftonville. In October 1894 it was renamed Hove and West Brighton, before being changed again to just Hove within a year.

This was not the original Hove station, however. This was opened in 1840 but closed when the Cliftonville Curve was constructed. The site was converted to Holland Road goods yard.

The supremacy of the railways began to be challenged with the advent of motor buses and cars. To try to combat this, the LB&SCR opened up halts in the ever-expanding urban area surrounding Brighton. In 1905 Holland Road Halt was opened. This was a short distance west of the original Hove station. Its service was mainly confined to rush hours by motor trains on stopping services to Worthing. The halt closed on 7 May 1956.

Another later addition came in 1887 in the form of the Devil's Dyke branch. It was built by the Brighton & Dyke Railway Company, but operated by the LB&SCR. This left the main line at a new halt, Aldrington Halt (originally Dyke Junction Halt), and was built to serve the growing tourist trade. The terminus was reached after a 3-mile climb up a 1-in-40 gradient to a height of 700 feet above sea level. There was an addition in 1891 after leaving Aldrington, and this was at Golf Club Halt. There was a bell in the bar of the clubhouse that sounded when the signal was pulled off at the terminus, which allowed the golf club members to finish their drinks in time to catch the train.

Another halt was opened in 1934. This was Rowan Halt, built to serve the new Aldrington housing estate.

For those venturing to the top, there was still a stiff half-mile hike to the summit after the 20-minute train journey. Various other attractions were installed at the top, including a steep-grade railway that ran down the north face of the hill towards Poynings, and an aerial cableway. This was only in operation from 1894 to 1909. It was 1,200 feet long and 200 feet high, spanning a valley to a neighbouring hill. The two cable cars could each carry four passengers, and it was worked by a diesel engine. Other attractions included two bandstands, fairground rides and a camera obscura. Initially trade had been good, peaking at the August bank holiday of 1893, when 30,000 people reached the summit by one means or another. After that it was financially in trouble and was in receivership from 1895 until it became part of the Southern Railway in 1923. The branch remained open until the end of 1938, after which holiday makers had to rely on a bus service.

Continuing along the west coast line, the next station to be reached is Portslade. When the line first opened it was known as 'Copperas Gap'. A lack of passenger traffic forced the station to close in 1847 and it remained closed for ten years. A new station building opened in 1881, which was built in the same Italianate style as many other LB&SCR buildings. In 1927, the name of the station was changed to Portlslade and West Hove.

The station also had a goods yard on the west side of the level crossing. It contained a holding pen for cattle bound for the nearby slaughterhouse. Cattle were often kept in these overnight and residents in nearby properties were sometimes kept awake by the bellowing of the distraught cattle. The goods yard survived until 1968.

The station has had more than its fair share of fatal accidents.

The terminus at Devils Dyke on 19 March 1927 with a Class E1, B113, in charge of a two-coach train, the first of which was a balloon coach – so called because of the shape of its roof. (H. C. Casserley)

This is the last passenger train on the Dyke Branch. It was in the hands of E4 tank No. 2480 on 31 December 1938. (WSCC Libraries)

Q class No. 30544 heads a Reading South–Brighton excursion passing through Portslade. (Edwin Wilmshurst)

In 1864 a Norwegian ship's captain, who had just docked at Shoreham, alighted at Portslade but from the wrong side of the train, and was hit by a passing express from Brighton. He was put on to the next train to Brighton in an attempt to get him to hospital but he died on the way. He is buried in Portslade cemetery.

Later that year another fatal accident occurred at the station when a train from Brighton overshot the platforms. The driver attempted to reverse up into the station, but one teenage passenger became impatient and tried to climb down from the train, but was crushed. At the young man's inquest, the driver was found to have been negligent.

In 1992 a man was killed when he jumped in front of the 07.47 fast train from Victoria to Portsmouth. In 2013 a passenger realised he was on the wrong platform and he crossed the railway line with his bags of shopping. The driver of the Worthing train that was in the station failed to see him as he pulled away and the passenger was crushed between train and platform.

Fishergate Halt was opened in 1905 and was served by motor trains to Worthing. This was soon followed by Southwick, where the original station buildings were replaced in the 1890s and then again in 1971.

Kingston Wharf was reached next, and this was built to serve the harbour at Shoreham, which not only handled freight traffic but had also been built to handle cross-Channel passenger traffic. Packet boats had left there for some time and by 1788, a regular service was operating. In 1847 the LB&SCR formed its own company to operate cross-Channel services, but they could not agree terms with the owners of Kingston Harbour, and so decided to build their own port at Newhaven. Kingston station closed in 1863. Although the port had closed for passenger traffic, it remained open for goods traffic, and the LB&SCR used it to bring coal ashore, building two coke ovens to provide fuel for their engines. The sidings on the wharf were not easily reached, being at a lower level than the tracks. An inclined plane had to be installed, with a turntable at either end to take wagons to and from the dockside. This was worked by a stationary engine attached to the wagons using chains. In 1938 the docks were rebuilt and a P class tank was used to haul wagons up the new 1-in-82 loop to meet the tracks. No. 1557 was the first loco to venture on to the docks. Eventually Class 03 shunters displaced the tank locos and they worked there until the docks closed in 1968.

In 1844, the Brighton & Chichester Railway sought powers to extend the railway from Shoreham to Chichester. The Duke of Norfolk, Earl of Arundel, was not best pleased as he owned the rights to ferry people across the River Adur. The original ferry had been replaced by a road bridge, on which a toll was charged. This was replaced by another sturdier structure in 1833. This lasted until 1923, when a steel bowstring-girder bridge was installed. The Shoreham & Chichester Railway, who were responsible for building the line, had to pay the Duke a sum of money to recompense him for the future loss of tolls. They also bought the old wooden bridge about a mile upstream from the newer one. The Shoreham–Horsham branch crosses the road here, and it was the crossing keeper's duty to collect tolls from motorists wishing to use the old bridge. In 1845 the company was granted powers to extend the line to Portsmouth and sell the completed line to the London & Brighton Railway.

The original railway bridge over the River Adur was reached from the east by an embankment rising for 600 yards and over nineteen brick arches, before crossing the river by the wooden trestle bridge. This bridge lasted for about fifty years until it needed to be replaced. A plate girder bridge was constructed, measuring 220 yards and resting on fourteen piers, and it is that one that survives today. When the west coast was reached, all the major works had been completed. The next 22 miles were fairly flat. Very few bridges were built, with roads being crossed using level crossings, meaning that many crossing keepers were employed. Many of these crossings still exist, which cause considerable delays today.

The line as far as Worthing opened on 24 November 1845, but only for single-track working while the navvies widened the embankment to allow for two tracks. On the opening day, one of the horses used to carry spoil away was spooked by a train and ran across the running line, causing a derailment. The train was pulled the rest of the way by three other horses.

In 1861, between Shoreham and Lancing, a junction was laid for a line through Steyning to Horsham, giving a secondary route to London. This will be covered later in this book.

There is one intermediate station, Lancing. The town was to become the site for the company's carriage and wagon works in 1912. Eastbourne had been the original choice for the carriage works but local opposition forced the LB&SCR to opt for their second choice, Lancing. The original site at Brighton had become very cramped and the 66-acre site at Lancing was purchased in 1910 for £21,683 2s 6d. Lancing had been a rural community before the works arrived, and there was a certain amount of hostility between the locals and the railwaymen that sometimes turned violent at the local hostelries. This waned when the local workforce, who had depended on the land to make a meagre existence, realised that working for the railway paid much better. Many employees moved from Brighton to Lancing with the works, but a special train ran daily to take workers between the works and Brighton. The LB&SCR were forced to run this train after industrial action by the workforce. It became known as 'The Lancing Belle'.

The works were the first in the country to employ a moving production line for repairing carriages. Different tasks were handled in different parts of the works, with the carriage travelling at about 6 inches per minute. In effect this meant that eight underframes complete with bogies could be manufactured every week.

The war kept the works busy. Shortages of petrol forced more people on to the railways, which also needed more stock to move supplies and troops. Many wagons were damaged by bombs and needed fixing, and new wagons had to be built as well to meet the demand. Employees were urged not to join the armed forces. Passenger carriages were converted into mobile ambulances, with whole trains being converted into mobile hospitals that included operating theatres. The works also diversified and built Bailey bridges and tail planes for Horsa gliders, while guns and ammunition were made in the machine shop. The works came under enemy attack on a few occasions with stock in the yard being damaged, but the works escaped relatively unscathed.

After the war an open day was held every year, with any profits being donated to the Southern Railway Servants Orphanage & Homes for the Elderly. These were held between 1949 and 1963.

At the Grouping in 1923, the three constituent companies each had their own wagon works. The other two were at Ashford and Eastleigh. The Southern Railway closed their works at Ashford, with most of their employees eventually moving to the Sussex coast. In the early days of British Railways the factory thrived and employed over 1,500 people. In 1962, however, it was decided to centralise all carriage and wagon building in one place and Lancing closed in favour of Eastleigh. Although this was put forward as an economic decision, it was in fact political. Lancing was a safe Conservative seat, whereas Eastleigh was marginal, and keeping the works there was seen as a vote winner. The works finally closed in 1965.

Billinton, the CME in 1913, put forward plans to move the locomotive works to Lancing as well, but the First World War intervened and the idea was dropped.

Another halt that opened in 1905 was Ham Bridge Halt. This was later changed to East Worthing.

The original station at Worthing was replaced in 1911. This was renamed Worthing Central in 1936 and was in fact the third station building. The previous ones were absorbed by the goods yard, which was fairly extensive. It also boasted locomotive watering facilities, which meant the construction of a water-softening plant. This was because the local water came from the chalky South Downs, leaving a build-up of calcium on surfaces with which it comes into contact.

The third station in Worthing is West Worthing, which opened on 4 November 1889. The station was part of a plan to develop the area as a holiday resort. A pier was planned at the end of Grand Avenue, and hotels were also planned. Directors, dignitaries and investors lunched at the West Worthing Golf Club, where plots of land were also

38 was a 4-4-2 class H1, built in 1905. In 1925 it was named *Portland Bill*. It lasted into BR days, when it was renumbered 32038, being withdrawn in July 1951. It was seen here at Worthing on an unknown date.

Class B2 4-4-0
No. 317 *Gerald Loder*
at Ford Junction with
a variety of stock on
2 February 1914.

auctioned off. Their plans fell foul not only of a financial crash in 1893, but also of a typhoid epidemic that broke out in Worthing. Not a single person visited the town in that year and it took some years for the town to recover. A large goods yard was built in the town in 1905 to cope with the produce from the market gardens that had grown up there. Some passenger services from Brighton terminated there and there was a reversing siding laid between the Up and Down roads to allow trains to turn round. In the 1930s a three-road carriage cleaning shed was built, using land from the goods yard.

A further 7.5 miles of track were opened on 16 March 1846, reaching Lyminster. It was initially called Littlehampton & Arundel. There were intermediate stations at Durrington-on-Sea, Goring-on-Sea and Angmering. Between Angmering and Ford lie the junctions that connect Littlehampton with the main line.

Class D1 No. 2229
at Bognor Regis
station. It was one
of an original batch
of 125 0-4-2 tank
engines introduced
by Stroudley
between 1873
and 1887.

Although it was built as double-tracked, it was run as a single-track line until 1847. In June of 1846 the line was opened as far as Chichester. It was also operated as single line until 1857, when the line was doubled. This section meant crossing the River Arun. This was originally achieved by a bridge with an opening span. This was replaced by a fixed-span bridge when the line was electrified in 1938. At first only one track was laid across it, but this was subsequently doubled, with facing points at either end. There were four intermediate stations – Ford (Ford Junction until 1923), Yapton, Woodgate (originally called Bognor, then Woodgate for Bognor) and Drayton. Woodgate and Yapton stations were closed in June 1864 when the branch to Bognor was opened. Drayton, which had been built to serve the nearby Goodwood racecourse, closed in 1930. Barnham was then reached and this became the junction for the branch to Bognor Regis, which opened on 1 June 1864. The original station was blown down in a storm in 1897 and its replacement burnt down two years later. The present station building dates from 1902. The line was originally a single-track branch, but this had been doubled by 1911 and electrified in the 1930s. The 'Regis' was only added in the 1930s after King George V spent some time there, recuperating from a serious illness.

K class No. 32344 and Q1 No. 33024 near Barnham on an Eastleigh–Newhaven freight. (Charlie Verrall)

Bognor with four un-rebuilt West Country/Battle of Britains – No. 34092 *City of Wells*, No. 34068 *Kenley*, No. 34087 *145 Squadron* and No. 34017 *lfracombe* – on shed. (Edwin Wilmshurst)

DS236 was a USA class tank, formerly numbered 30074, that worked at Lancing Carriage Works between 1963 and 1965, when it was scrapped. It replaced Class A1 DS680 (below) that had worked there since 1932 and AIX DS681, formerly No. 32659, which joined it in 1953.

'The Lancing Belle', headed by E4s Nos 32503 and 32468, passes Portslade and West Hove. (Edwin Wilmshurst)

Inside Lancing Works, A1X DS1 poses in front of a balloon coach being used as a storeroom. (Edwin Wilmshurst)

Not strictly relevant in a book on steam, but interesting anyway – DS499 was a petrol-engine shunter used in the carriage works. (Edwin Wilmshurst)

Chichester is reached after continuing along the main line from Barnham. This used to be the junction for the branch northwards through Midhurst, which opened in 1881, and the terminus of the Selsey Tramway, which was closed in 1935. The station could once boast a goods yards with cattle docks.

The Hundred of Manhood & Selsey Tramway opened in 1897 as far as Selsey Town, with a short extension to Selsey Beach the following year. It was built to standard gauge by Colonel Stephens as a tramway, and so it did not need to comply with regulations that covered railways. Although fairly popular before the First World War, it suffered from competition with the motor car. To try to save money, it changed from being steam-operated to petrol-driven rail cars, but it was not enough to save the railway, which closed in January 1935.

After leaving Chichester, the line passes through Bosham before entering Hampshire.

Construction continued westwards, and Havant was reached in March 1857 and Portsmouth in June the same year.

Selsey Tramway 2-4-2T No. 2 *Selsey* with three carriages. (The John Law Collection)

With the spire of Chichester Cathedral in the background, S15 No. 30843 passes slowly on 10 May 1964. (Trevor Tupper)

A view of Chichester, looking east, as the 11.10 Plymouth–Brighton service with Std Class 4 2-6-4 tank No. 80014 passes through on 16 April 1964. (Trevor Tupper)

West Sussex Secondary Lines

Chichester to Midhurst and Hardham Junction

On 7 July 1881 the LB&SCR opened a new line that left their coastal route at Fishbourne, just west of Chichester, and went north through Lavant, Singleton and Cocking to join up with the line from Horsham to Petersfield at Midhurst. The line was originally going to be extended to Haslemere but the recession of 1866 put an end to this proposal.

There had been various schemes put forward, but wealthy landowners in the area had made unreasonable requests, e.g., that lines crossing their estates must be in tunnels. The financial crash of the 1860s intervened and all plans for a railway were shelved. A proposal by the SER to build a line from Dorking to Midhurst had sparked the LB&SCR into purchasing the land between Chichester and Midhurst but the financial crash of 1866 had put work on hold, and the powers granted under the Chichester & Midhurst Railway Act of 1864 eventually dissolved. A similar Act was granted in 1877, with the LB&SCR given four years to complete the work.

LB&SCR Class B2 4-4-0 locomotive No. 315 *Duncannon* being topped up with water at Chichester.

Steep gradients, deep cuttings and tunnels made the line very expensive to build. It was single-track but much of the earthworks could have accommodated double track.

When the line was originally opened, trains left from their own bay platform at Chichester and ran on a track running parallel to the Portsmouth line as far as Fishbourne, where it diverted to the north. It was some time later before a junction was installed.

Lavant station, the first station to be reached journeying north, was built in the country-house style, similar to many designed by T. H. Myres of the LB&SCR. It was built on land owned by the Duke of Richmond, who decreed that all passenger trains must stop there. It opened in July 1881, but was never a financial success and closed in July 1935. A siding was constructed some years later to serve a nearby gravel pit. General freight continued until 1968, and sugar beet continued until 1970. The gravel pit south of the station continued to be served by the railways until 1991. The trackbed is now part of the Centurion Way cycle path.

The next station up the line was Singleton. West Dean tunnel, measuring 445 yards, was situated between the stations. Singleton was the closest station to Goodwood horse-racing track and had to cater for thousands of racegoers, and so it was built on a different scale to other stations on the line. It boasted four platforms joined by an underpass, two signal boxes and enough sidings to store fourteen trains of carriages and horseboxes. Even this was sometimes not enough, and sidings at Lavant had to be used. There was even a refreshment room with a long marble-topped counter and stained-glass windows, in keeping with the expectations of the upper classes and even royalty that used the facilities.

LB&SCR class B2 B321 near Chichester, *c.* 1925. The 'B' before the number was added in Southern days and indicated that Brighton was responsible for its maintenance – 'A' stood for Ashford and 'E' for Eastleigh.

As part of the Vectis Farewell railtour on 3 October 1965, Q1s Nos 33027 and 33020 worked from Chichester up to Lavant and back.

Lavant was a grand station for a rural location. C2X No. 32548 was pictured with a local goods train for Chichester on 3 August 1955. (Edwin Wilmshurst)

Another local goods service arrives at Lavant, this time on 8 April 1959 with E4 No. 32495 in charge. (Trevor Tupper)

Leaving Singleton, the summit of the line was reached before Singleton and Cocking tunnels were negotiated (741 yards and 738 yards respectively) and Cocking station reached. The line then continued to Midhurst, which had already been reached by two other railways. The L&SWR was the first to arrive in 1864 with a line from Petersfield. The L&SWR had taken over the Petersfield Railway by the time the line opened. Neither of the railway companies was allowed to run over each other's lines. Indeed they each built their own station, which were 11 chains (242 yards) apart. There was a length of track in between, but this ran over a weak bridge, and locos were not allowed to run across it. Through passengers had to walk between the two, but goods wagons could be horse-drawn over the bridge.

Petersfield is in Hampshire but the two intermediate stations are in Sussex. These are Rogate and Elsted, both over a mile from the villages they served. Rogate had a siding for a brickworks and originally two platform faces, whereas Elsted had only one platform and a two-road goods yard. Although they were not financially viable, they stayed open into BR days but both passenger and freight services were withdrawn completely on 7 May 1955.

The LB&SCR arrived in 1866, when their line from Pulborough via Petworth was opened. When the branch from Chichester opened, the track layout was altered and a new station building was opened even further away from their rivals. It stayed that way until the Southern Railway took over, and the old L&SWR station was closed in 1925 in favour of the ex-LB&SCR one.

The line had never been a financial success and the increase in use of private motors and more convenient bus services led to all passenger services being withdrawn in July 1935. Freight traffic continued with a daily goods service. Tunnels on the line were used in the Second World War to store ammunition trains, and doors were even fitted to either end of Singleton and Cocking tunnels.

In 1951 a severe storm washed away the trackbed just south of Midhurst, leaving the rails suspended in mid-air. The crew of an approaching goods train failed to notice this until it was too late. Although they jumped clear, their steed, a C2X, No. 32522, plunged down the 20-foot gap. It took three months to rescue the locomotive, while the damage to the track was so severe that it was decided that it would be uneconomical to repair.

The ex-LB&SCR section east of Midhurst also closed for passengers in May 1955, but remained open for freight from Pulborough until September 1964. There had been three through stations between Midhurst and the line from Littlehampton to Horsham, which it joined at Hardham Junction. These were Selham, Petworth and Fittleworth. Selham station opened in July 1872, six years after the line opened. Petworth was the terminus of the line for seven years. It was actually 1.5 miles from the town and a horse cab had to be taken to finish the journey. The line had reached here from Horsham in 1859, but the section to Midhurst was not completed until 1866. It comprised a single platform but had a passing loop for goods trains. Fittleworth station, a single platform with no passing loop but a two-track goods yard, never opened until September 1889, and it closed for passenger traffic at the same time as other stations on the line. Freight traffic was withdrawn in 1963, however – three years before the line closed.

Slightly out of our area but heading our way was the RCTS 'Hampshireman' railtour at Petersfield on 6 February 1955 with T9s Nos 30301 and 30732 in charge.

Right: Q class No. 30530 heads an RCTS railtour, 'The Midhurst Belle', through Petworth on 18 October 1964. (Keith Harwood)

Below: No. 32503, an E4 0-6-2 designed by R. J. Billington and introduced in 1910, stops at Selham while working the LCGB Sussex Coast railtour on 24 June 1962.

Working the same section of the Sussex Coast railtour with No. 32503 was Class E6 No. 32417, also at Selham.

On 6 February 1955, the RCTS ran a tour called 'The Hampshireman', hauled by two class E5xs, Nos 32576 and 32570. It stopped here at Midhurst, where many of enthusiasts took the opportunity to photograph the occasion, including one gent who saw fit to scale the signal for a better view!

Midhurst station sees the arrival of LB&SCR Class D1 tank No. 34 *Balham*.

East of Fittleworth is Hardham Junction, where the line joins the track up from Littlehampton. This latter line was not opened until 1863, four years after what was to become the branch to Petworth.

Littlehampton to Horsham and Three Bridges

The Littlehampton station that exists today was not the first one. That was a small station on the Brighton–Portsmouth line, called Arundel and Littlehampton. The present station opened in 1863 when a branch from Ford reached the town. The original station on the line then closed. Junctions were formed that allowed running from Littlehampton eastwards to Brighton, northwards to Horsham and London, and westwards to Portsmouth.

A harbour was built, with a railway line running along the wharf. Not only were goods unloaded there – mainly from France – but passenger ferries also left for France, the Channel Islands and the Isle of Wight. The port lost much of its trade when Newhaven Harbour opened.

The line was electrified in 1938, which meant that the locomotive shed was no longer needed and it closed. Goods traffic continued until 1970. The station still has facilities to stable, wash and clean the electric units stored there overnight.

LB&SCR A1X No. 653 in Southern livery at Littlehampton on 10 April 1926.

K class No. 32353 leaving Arundel with the 'Sussex Coast Limited' LCGB railtour, 24 June 1962. (Charlie Verrall)

The line north followed the course of the River Arun, and so became known as the Arun Valley Line. Arundel station is the first station up the line to Horsham and Three Bridges. It was opened on 3 August 1863. Until then, Arundel had been a port on the River Arun, but the coming of the railway put an end to the town as a port. The station was just south of the town and had a large goods shed within the goods yard.

Amberley is the next station along the line. This is the site of Amberley Museum and Heritage Centre, formerly called the Chalk Pits Museum; the 36-acre site used to be a chalk quarry where the chalk mined was converted into lime for use in mortar and cement. This was then transported by rail.

Hardham Junction was then crossed, where the line from Midhurst joined before Pulborough station was reached. It first opened in 1859 as a station on the route to Petworth. It had to wait four years to become a junction with the line from the South Coast. The former line closed to passengers in 1955 and all goods services were cut in the 1960s. One of the three platform faces was reserved for the Petworth line and this has since been lifted, making Pulborough another simple two-road station.

Billingshurst opened in 1859 with other stations on the line. It could only handle four-coach trains until 2006, when the platforms were extended to handle eight-coach trains. The signal box was thought to be one of the oldest operational boxes still in use, dating from 1876. It was the only remaining Saxby & Farmer Type 1b box. It closed on 14 March 2014, when Three Bridges took over the signalling of the line. It was dismantled and taken to Amberley Museum. John Saxby had been employed in Brighton Works, and became interested in signalling. He designed his own interlocking system and set up in business manufacturing them at Haywards Heath. He was joined by John Farmer, who was LB&SCR's assistant traffic manager.

April 1962 sees an M7 arriving at Christ's Hospital with a local passenger train. (H. C. Casserley)

Ex-L&SWR T9 No. 120 in original livery entering Christ's Hospital with a LCGB railtour on 24 June 1962.

Nos 32503 and 32417 near Itchingfield Junction with the same railtour on 24 June 1962. (Charlie Verrall)

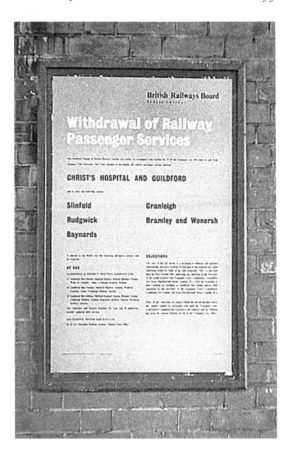

Closure notice posted on Christ's
Hospital station for the line to Guildford.
(Keith Harwood)

Continuing our journey north, Itchingfield Junction is then crossed where the line from Shoreham via Steyning joins, before Christ's Hospital station is reached. The school had opened in London in the sixteenth century to educate the children of the city's poor, but in 1902 new premises were opened just outside Horsham. A splendid new station was built to serve the school, consisting of no less than seven platforms. It was only after the station was finished that the school decided that it would be completely for boarding pupils, so the expected daily influx of pupils never materialised. It did mean, however, that at the start of terms many pupils arrived carrying a lot of baggage so facilities were included for unloading luggage vans for the pupils. The station is now just another bland through station with two platforms. The line also diverged here with a line turning north to Guildford through Slinfold, Rudgwick, Baynards, Cranleigh and Bramley & Wonersh. The single-track line was opened on 2 October 1885, built by the Guildford & Horsham Direct Railway. Another scheme had been put forward to link the two towns by draining the Wey & Arun Canal and building a railway on the canal bed, but this scheme was soon dropped.

Slinfold was the first station up the line, which had a small goods yard serving a brickworks and timber yard. Rudgwick was similar, with a small two-road goods yard. The border with Surrey is then crossed. The whole line closed on 14 June 1965 as one of the Beeching cuts.

Ivatt 2-6-2T at Slinfold in the winter of 1962. (Keith Harwood)

Another shot of 'The Hampshireman' tour of 1955, seen previously at Midhurst. This time it is pictured at Horsham.

Another railtour at Horsham was the SLS special on 3 May 1953, with Class H2 No. 32425 *Trevose Head* in charge.

Fairburn 2-6-4T No. 42080 takes on water at Horsham on 14 April 1951 with the 18.15 Epsom–Brighton passenger service.

Left: A Class I3 tank was seen entering
Horsham on 30 August 1930 with a
Saturday-only Portsmouth Harbour–
London Bridge service.

Below: With the roundhouse in the
background, Class E4 No. 32470 was
seen taking water at Horsham shed in
1958. (Ernie's Railway Archive)

Horsham shed played host to Tonbridge-based Class H No. 31543 in 1958. (Ernie's Railway Archive)

Still at Horsham shed in 1958, where Maunsell's N class No. 31839 is ready for its next turn. (Ernie's Railway Archive)

A general view of Horsham shed on 8 August 1959 with Class 700 No. 30350 and E4 No. 32469. (John Scrace)

Horsham is one of Sussex's larger inland towns, and had a station and goods facilities to match. The station opened in 1848 and was a terminus on the line from Three Bridges. It was enlarged several times, as it became an important junction with lines radiating north through Surrey to Guildford and Dorking, west to Petersfield and south to Shoreham and Littlehampton.

When the line was electrified in 1938, a new 'modern' structure was built, which is nowadays Grade II listed. The station lost some of its importance when, in 1955, the line to Petersfield closed and in the mid-1960s when the lines to Guildford and Shoreham also closed.

After leaving Horsham, Littlehaven is reached. It did not open until 1907 and was called Rusper Road Halt before being changed to Littlehaven Crossing Halt and then Littlehaven Halt within a year of opening.

There was another station that opened in 1907 – Roffey Road Halt – but this closed in 1937 due to lack of trade.

Ifield station was opened in June 1907. It was originally called Lyons Crossing Halt for a year before becoming Ifield Halt, being served by rail motor trains. It changed to Ifield in 1930.

Faygate, another simple two-road station, is then passed through before Crawley is reached. Crawley expanded rapidly during the 1950/60s and a new station opened in 1968, funded by a six-storey development above it. The next station is Three Bridges on the main line to Brighton, which has been described in an earlier chapter.

Crawley station, as a C2X passes on a rather murky day in March 1960. (WSCC Libraries)

On 13 June 1965, the LCGB ran their 'Wealdsman' railtour with a variety of locomotives. It was booked for a photo stop at Steyning between 18.15–18.30 on a leg from Haywards Heath via Hove and Shoreham to Horsham, before handing over to Nos 33027/33006 for the trip back to Waterloo.

The Adur Valley Line

As mentioned in a previous paragraph, Itchingfield Junction saw the line from Steyning and Shoreham join the line from Midhurst. It left the Brighton–Portsmouth line just west of Shoreham. It opened in 1861 and was known as the Adur Valley line. It had been constructed in response to a proposal by the LSWR to extend their territory via a line via Dorking and Horsham to Chichester and Shoreham. The London & Brighton (Steyning Branch) Railway Act received Royal Assent in 1846. The company merged later that year to become part of the LB&SCR. The L&SWR then dropped its plans, while financial problems forced the LB&SCR to put their plans on hold as well. It was not until 1856 that the Steyning Railway company was formed by a group of influential residents who offered to build the line and lease it to the LB&SCR. However, they failed to raise the finance needed and the LB&SCR refused to invest, so the scheme was abandoned. The following year a new scheme was put forward by the Shoreham, Horsham & Dorking Railway. This prompted the LB&SCR to revive plans for a railway. With two schemes on the table, a parliamentary enquiry was held to determine which should proceed, with the LB&SCR winning the day, as it was thought that the latter would probably extend their line to Guildford.

Beeding, on the banks of the River Adur, was soon reached. It never had a station but it did have a large cement works with its own narrow-gauge railway.

Bramber station was the first stop encountered. Although the village it served was only small, the nearby Bramber Castle attracted many visitors and excursion trains, so the platforms were built to be long enough to accommodate these.

Aveling & Porter No. 4612 at Beeding Cement Works. (E. H. C. Shorto, IRS collection)

W. Bagnall No. 2262 *Capstan II* at Beeding Cement Works. The limestone quarry opened in 1851 and production finished in 1991, with the buildings and plant just left to decay. (IRS collection)

Class E4 0-6-2T No. 32580 takes water at Steyning. (Edwin Wilmshurst)

Steyning was the next stop and was the location for a weekly auction, which led to a lot of agricultural traffic being carried. Henfield was then reached, which was a simple through station but had sidings mainly for delivery of coal to keep the steam mill and gas works fed.

Partridge Green and West Grinstead were the next two stations. The latter saw a lot of horse traffic due to the nearby national stud and hunt kennels. Although the buildings have been demolished, the platforms still exist and the local council have erected a replica station name board.

Southwater was the site for a brickworks, so the goods yard saw a lot of coal being delivered to power the kilns and the majority of the bricks were taken away by rail. Itchingfield Junction was then reached and the line from Petworth was joined.

Ernest Marples, the Minister of Transport, proposed closing the line in 1963, but local opposition was great and effective, with 289 objections being lodged and a public enquiry held. They argued that the proposed replacement bus service would be much more time-consuming and could not replace the train service; the Transport Users Consultative Committee agreed with them. This was borne out by the fact that a replacement bus service run by Southdown had to be withdrawn due to lack of use.

A change of government did little to safeguard the line, and in 1965 the Labour Party put forward further proposals to close the line, along with other closures recommended by Lord Beeching. It finally closed in 1966 and the track bed was lifted soon afterwards. It now forms part of the Downs Link footpath.

Class D1 0-4-2T No. 2625 at Partridge Green on a Horsham–Brighton stopping service.

Ivatt 2 6-2T No. 41301 stops at Partridge Green on a Horsham–Brighton service. (Edwin Wilmshurst)

The 'Wealdsman' railtour of 13 June 1965 stops at Forest Row for a photo opportunity. In charge of this leg were U class No. 31803 and N class No. 31411.

K class No. 32353 double-heads with a sister engine, pulling a goods train at Rowfant.

Rowfant was the location of H class No. 31263 on a Three Bridges–East Grinstead passenger service on 26 May 1963. (Ernie's Railway Archive)

Three Bridges to Tunbridge Wells West

The East Grinstead Railway was formed in 1852 to build a line from Three Bridges to East Grinstead, a distance of just under 7 miles. Before the line was finished, permission had been granted to extend the line to Tunbridge Wells West.

The branch line left Three Bridges to the east, travelling through north Sussex. The first station was Rowfant, opening with the line in 1855. It was built to serve two influential gentlemen – Curtis Miranda Lampson, who was vice chairman of the Atlantic Telegraph Company, and a wealthy fur trader who lived in Rowfant and owned the land upon which the railway was to be built. He sold the land cheaply to the railway company on the proviso that a station was built and he could stop any train on request. The other nearby resident of Worth Hall was a LB&SCR director, John Nix.

Rowfant shared with Kingscote the dubious distinction of being the LB&SCR station that took the least in passenger revenues. In the late 1950s, the station received a boost when aviation fuel was stored there, with stocks being replenished by rail.

Grange Road was the next station along the line but this did not open until 1860. It had a small goods yard, which was operational until October 1961.

East Grinstead was reached on 1 October 1866. Stations on the route were Forest Row, Hartfield and Withyham. There have been three stations at East Grinstead, with the initial one being at Swan Mead, off the London Road.

Std Class 4 2-6-4T No. 80033 heading north at East Grinstead low level on 30 April 1955 while a train for Tunbridge Wells waits at the high-level station.

H class 0-4-4T No. 31308
at East Grinstead high level
on 10 June 1961. The poster
on the wall advertises future
matches to be played by
Brighton & Hove Albion.
(Ian D. Nolan)

When, in 1862, parliamentary approval was given to build a line from Tunbridge Wells West to Groombridge, forming a junction at East Grinstead, a new station had to be built. This was located a few yards north of the original one, being situated in a cutting with the station buildings located on an overbridge. The original station site became the location of the goods yard. When the Lewes & East Grinstead Railway and the Croydon, Oxted & East Grinstead Railway arrived in 1882, running north–south rather than east–west, there was not enough room to form a junction without purchasing a nearby timber yard, which the LB&SCR was not prepared to do. It was decided to re-site the station 300 yards west from the existing one and build it on two levels with the east–west line running above the north–south line. This station opened on 15 October 1883, with the main station buildings being on the lower level.

The line from East Grinstead to Tunbridge Wells was never as well patronised as the line from Three Bridges. There were three intermediate stations. The first of these was

Class C2X No. 32539 at East
Grinstead, heading towards
Lewes on 30 April 1955.

Forest Row. This was a simple two-road station with a small goods yard. Freight services lasted at the station until November 1966.

Next along the line was Hartfield. This was a single-track station with an overbridge. The station buildings still exist and are in use as a private dwelling.

Withyham station was a single-platform station with a typical LB&SCR country house-style station and signal box adjacent to the crossing gates.

The county border with Kent was then crossed and Groombridge and High Rocks Halt were then passed through before arriving at Tunbridge Wells West.

Tank engines were mainly used to run the passenger services, initially with Stroudley's D1s and sometimes B1 Gladstones. These were superseded by Billinton's E4 and E5 tanks. I3s could also be seen on services to and from London. In Southern days, the later N and U 2-6-0s could also put in appearances. In BR days Fairburn 2-6-4 tanks and Standard 2-6-4 tanks were also regular operators on services.

The line was a victim of the Beeching cuts and closed in January 1967. Much of the track bed between East Grinstead and Three Bridges has been turned into a cycle path called the Worth Way. The trackbed from East Grinstead to Groombridge has been opened as a public footpath and cycle path called the Forest Way, and the line from Tunbridge Wells West to Eridge via High Rocks and Groombridge has been reopened as a preserved Spa Valley Railway.

Withyham signal box was dismantled and rebuilt at Sheffield Park station on the Bluebell Railway.

Withyham station was the last one to be encountered before crossing the border into Kent.

H class No. 31308 passing a 'Whistle' sign at High Rocks on 16 June 1962.

Class E4 No. 32517 at Tunbridge Wells West, just outside our area but heading our way. This station is now part of the Spa Valley railway.

The East Coast Route

Lines leaving Brighton to the east served the seaside towns of Hastings, Eastbourne, Seaford and Newhaven, as well as inland towns of Tunbridge Wells and Uckfield, which left the coastal route at Lewes. The suburb of Brighton called Kemp Town was also served by a short branch.

Through services from west to east and vice versa were very limited as there was only one platform in Brighton station that was able to serve either direction. This was Platform 3 and the pointwork leading west was within the platforms, and only a four-coach train could be accommodated. Longer trains would have to reverse at Preston Park and take the Cliftonville Curve.

Construction of the line to the east was undertaken by the Brighton, Lewes & Hastings Railway and opened on 8 June 1846, which was the same day as the first day of the service westwards as far as Chichester. It was reported in the *Brighton Herald* that three trains left the station at the same time – inaugural trains to Chichester and Lewes as well as a train to London.

Inhabitants of Lewes were apparently not as excited to see the first train arrive as those of Brighton were to see it leave. Many inhabitants were against the railway and carried

Within twenty-four hours of a direct hit, the trains were running again. I cannot see the Health & Safety Executive allowing trains to run in these circumstances today! Class E4 No. 32475, with the driver looking anxiously from his cab, approaches Brighton from Lewes.

on using the stagecoach services. Many were unhappy because of a lack of consultation of the siting of the station and thought that the route taken, which ran through land owned by a company director, was questionable. This deviation from the desired route meant that the line carrying on towards Hastings had to leave via a bend that was of 'fearful and suspect character'.

Returning to Brighton, the lines to the east left from the higher numbered platforms adjacent to the new workshops. Immediately leaving Brighton, the line crossed the impressive London Road Viaduct built by John Urpeth Rastrick, who also designed the Ouse Valley Viaduct. Indeed the two structures show many similarities, including the pierced piers. They are both now Grade II* listed structures. It is 1,200 feet long and is 67 feet high at its maximum and built on a sharp curve. Most of the piers are 7 feet thick at the base but only 5 feet thick at the top, but the one spanning the road measures 22 feet thick at the base and 19.5 feet thick at the top. The twenty-seven brick-built arches used 10 million bricks and took under a year to build. The foundation stone was laid by John Rastrick on 29 May 1845 and it was ready for the grand opening the following year. When constructed, it crossed open countryside apart from one span that crossed a road. This is now the A23 out of Brighton and the arch that spans the road is of a wider dimension than the rest. Brighton was expanding rapidly at the time and it was not long before the area beneath the viaduct was built up with many back-to-back streets, many of which housed those working on the railway in various tasks.

A view of the viaduct with A1X No. 32636 and E6 No. 32418 approaching Brighton from Lewes. (Charlie Verrall)

On 25 May 1943 it was hit by a German bomb, one of a string dropped by a Focke-Wulf, which completely destroyed two arches and one pier. Incredibly the viaduct was temporarily repaired within twenty-four hours and had rail services running over it again.

Immediately over the viaduct is London Road station. This was not opened until October 1877. This was because on the opening of the railway this was unspoilt countryside; however, by 1877, Brighton had expanded greatly and the area was fully developed. After leaving London Road on the way to Lewes, the track enters the short Ditchling Road tunnel. The line to Kemp Town leaves at Kemp Town Junction after leaving the tunnel.

The Kemp Town branch was the most heavily engineered line for its length in the country. It took five years to build at a cost of over £100,000, which paid for a 1,024-yard tunnel through Race Hill and a fourteen-arch viaduct, as well as embankments and other smaller bridges. It was not built as a financially viable project, but more to deter the London, Chatham & Dover Railway, who wanted to build their own terminus at Kemp Town.

An intermediate station at Lewes Road was opened on 1 September 1873 and Hartington Road Halt on 1 January 1906. The halt only lasted for five years, closing in 1911. Lewes Road had an island platform as well as the platform adjacent to the main buildings. Kemp Town station was a substantial building, designed by David Mocatta, but only had one platform for passengers, although it did have an extensive goods yard.

On Saturday 12 January 1963 the morning goods train, which arrived around 8.20 a.m., came out of the tunnel and its wheels started spinning on the icy rails. The loco failed to stop and crashed through the buffers and platform, coming to rest in an office,

Class C2X No. 32539 passes Kemp Town Junction on 8 November 1948 with the 09.48 Brighton–Tunbridge Wells stopping service.

which it demolished. Both driver and fireman were taken to hospital but recovered. The fireman was killed at Itchingfield Junction the following year, when the loco he was firing also crashed.

The line was never going to be attractive to passengers, being a circuitous route to cover a small distance. Road transport became even more attractive, with the introduction of buses and trolleybuses to the town centre being not only quicker but also cheaper. The line therefore closed to passengers at the end of 1932, but freight traffic continued until 1971. There were a number of enthusiasts' specials over the line and, on the last day of service, a three-car diesel multiple unit ran a shuttle service to Brighton. After closure the line was bought by Brighton Corporation, who wasted no time in lifting the tracks and demolishing the buildings. The northern end of the tunnel has been blocked up but the southern end is still open, albeit as part of an industrial estate, which is not accessible to the public.

The viaduct over Hartington Road was demolished in 1973 and the longer one over the Lewes Road in 1976. There are now no traces that the line ever existed.

Continuing the journey towards Lewes, a new station stands at Moulscombe. It was opened in May 1980 and was built not only to serve the nearby housing estate with the same name, but also the nearby University of Sussex.

The original Falmer station was built in 1848, about a mile to the east of its present location, but was re-sited in 1866 to be nearer the village it served. It received a boost in trade when the universities of Sussex and Brighton opened nearby. A further boost occurred when Brighton and Hove Albion football club opened their new stadium nearby. Passenger numbers nearly doubled between 2005 and 2014, with over 0.25 million

To celebrate the centenary of Brighton Works an enthusiasts' special was run; it was pictured here at Kemp Town on 19 October 1952 with AIX No. 32636 in charge.

Class A1 No. 81 at Kemp Town. The loco had been temporarily converted to 2-4-0 between September 1905 and February 1913. (John Law Collection)

passengers being carried. Extra trains are laid on for match days, and the platforms had to be extended to accommodate these.

Lewes was then entered from the south-west direction. At this time it was a terminus at Friars Walk, but it evolved into a junction with routes coming from five directions – Brighton from the west, Haywards Heath and London from the north, Eastbourne from the east and Newhaven/Seaford from the south, which all still exist. There used to be another route that left via a bridge over the High Street to Uckfield and Tunbridge Wells.

The line from Haywards Heath leaves the Brighton main line just south of Wivelsfield at Keymer Junction, serving Plumpton and Cooksbridge before reaching Lewes. The construction of the line was authorised in 1845 to the Brighton, Lewes & Hastings Railway but, on the opening of the line on 1 October 1847, it was purchased by the LB&SCR. Plumpton station was not opened until June 1863. It was not only built to serve the village of Plumpton Green, but also the racecourse, which is adjacent to the station.

It has recently been the subject of much local controversy, because the road through the village that crosses the railway line did so by the original crossing gates that were controlled by the signal box next to the gates. The signal box had been given Grade II listed building status. However, Network Rail closed the crossing in September 2015, saying the gates needed to be replaced. Lewes District Council objected, saying that replacing the gates with lifting barriers would cause 'substantial harm to the significance of the signal box'. The road remained closed, splitting the village in two and forcing a 7-mile detour to the other side of the gates while the dispute continued. Network Rail eventually won the argument, and lifting barriers were installed, which are controlled from Three Bridges.

Cooksbridge is the other intermediate station. It was originally called Cooks Bridge but was never a financial success. When the line first opened, only two London-bound trains per day stopped there. In the 1950s it had an hourly service on the Seaford–Horsted

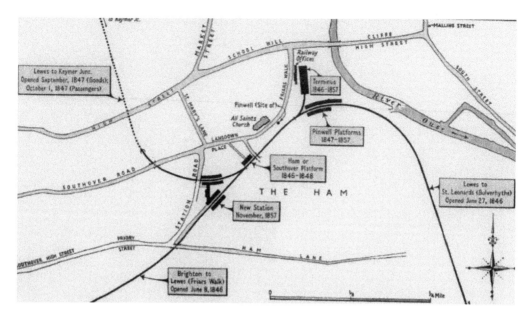

Map showing the various stations at Lewes before the tracks were remodelled.

Keynes service and, apart from peak periods, for anyone wishing to go to London, a change at Haywards Heath was required.

Lewes is reached via a 396-yard tunnel on a very sharp curve. The station building must rank as one of the finest in the region. It was designed by F. D. Brick and is similar in design to Eastbourne, except that the main entrance is on a road overbridge with a footbridge spanning the triangular-shaped platforms.

The line from Hastings was opened about three weeks after the Brighton line opened, but it met the latter at a point just west of the station, with a new platform called 'Ham' opening.

The line from Keymer Junction arrived the following year, and new platforms were built and called Pinwell. In 1857 a new station was built, which lasted until 1889 when the current station was opened.

This new station consists of five platforms, with Nos 1 and 2 serving the lines to London and the other three the coastal services. There used to be a single track between the present platforms 3 and 5, with access either side of the train, but this has been filled in.

The station was severely flooded in November 1960, and again in October 2000, with the entire trackbed under about 2 feet of water on both occasions.

The tracks leaving eastwards diverge outside the town at Southerham Junction, with a branch heading south to serve the port of Newhaven and the town of Seaford. Newhaven was reached in 1847, with Seaford having to wait a while longer. The Newhaven & Seaford Railway had been authorised to build the line from Newhaven to Seaford, but the operation of the branch was always going to be the responsibility of the LB&SCR. The Seaford extension was not opened until 1 June 1864. A horse-drawn bus service had been introduced in 1862 from Seaford to connect with the trains from

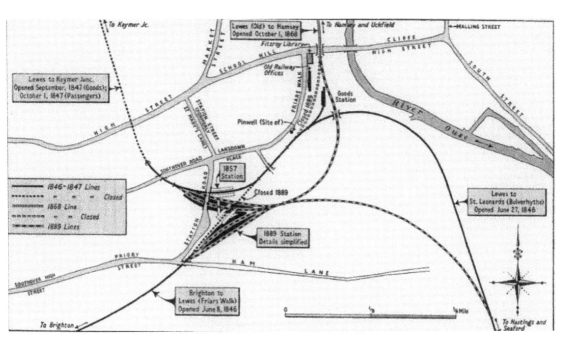

Above: Map of the revised layout of Lewes station, showing the original and revised curves leaving to the east. The original curve became part of the goods yard.

Right: On 27 September 1857 at Lewes, Craven 2-4-0 No. 174's boiler blew up. It had been built in 1864 and rebuilt in 1871. It survived the explosion, being renumbered 488 in 1881 and 454 in 1887. It was scrapped in 1889.

A panorama of Lewes station, taken from the northern end as the lines from Haywards Heath and London enter the station. The lines to the left, which served the goods yard, have since been lifted and the area now forms part of the car park.

LB&SCR 0-4-2 locomotive No. 185 takes water at Lewes, heading for Newhaven or Eastbourne. Two cattle wagons sit at the cattle dock.

Class I3 No. 32075 waits at Lewes on 16 May 1951.

On 7 October 1962, the RCTS ran a railtour through Sussex. AIX No. 32636 headed E6 No. 32418 through Lewes on its way from Brighton to Newhaven. (Ben Brooksbank)

With the chalk cliffs in the background, Class C2X No. 32441 enters Lewes with a northbound freight on 30 April 1955.

Above: On the same day as the previous image, ex-LMS 2-6-4T No. 42101 enters Lewes with an Oxted–Brighton service.

Left: A flier issued by British Railways, offering passport-free day trips from Newhaven to Dieppe and Paris – even if it did mean changing from boat to train at 3 o'clock in the morning!

BRITISH RAILWAYS

"NO PASSPORT" EXCURSIONS TO
DIEPPE and PARIS
VIA
LONDON · NEWHAVEN · DIEPPE

MONDAYS TUESDAYS & WEDNESDAYS
11th JULY to 14th SEPTEMBER inclusive

A WHOLE DAY IN THE FRENCH CAPITAL

TIME TABLE

OUTWARDS					
WOLVERHAMPTON Low Level	.. dep.	4.35 pm.			
BIRMINGHAM Snow Hill	.. dep.	5. 0 pm.	..	..	
LEAMINGTON SPA General ..	.. dep.	5.28 pm.	..	..	
BANBURY General	.. dep.		..	..	5.17 pm.
WORCESTER Foregate Street	.. dep.		..	4.42 pm.	
WORCESTER Shrub Hill	.. dep.		..	4.55 pm.	
OXFORD ..	.. dep.		..	6.20 pm.	
READING General	.. dep.		6.37 pm.		
LONDON Paddington ..	.. arr.	7.15 pm.	7.20 pm.	7.27 pm.	7.35 pm.
LONDON Victoria	.. dep.		9. 5 pm.		
NEWHAVEN Harbour ..	{ arr.		10.14 pm.		
	{ dep.		10.55 pm.		
DIEPPE Maritime ..	{ arr.		2.50 am.		
	{ dep.		3.36 am.		
PARIS St. Lazare ..	.. arr.		6.12 am.		
RETURN (on day of arrival)					
PARIS St. Lazare ..	.. dep.		10. 3 pm.		
DIEPPE Maritime ..	{ arr.		12.35 am.		
	{ dep.		1.20 am.		
NEWHAVEN Harbour ..	{ arr.		5.20 am.		
	{ dep.		6. 9 am.		
LONDON Victoria ..	.. arr.		7.20 am.		
LONDON Paddington ..	.. dep.	9.10 am.		9.15 am.	
READING General ..	.. arr.			9.53 am.	
OXFORD ..	.. arr.			10.32 am.	
WORCESTER Shrub Hill ..	.. arr.			12. 0 noon	
WORCESTER Foregate Street ..	.. arr.			12. 6 pm.	
BANBURY General ..	.. arr.	10.39 am.		..	
LEAMINGTON SPA General ..	.. arr.	11. 6 am.		..	
BIRMINGHAM Snow Hill ..	.. arr.	11.44 am.		..	
WOLVERHAMPTON Low Level ..	.. arr.	12. 8 pm.		..	

PASSENGERS CROSS LONDON AT THEIR OWN EXPENSE
THERE IS A FREQUENT SERVICE OF UNDERGROUND TRAINS (Circle Line)

ACCOMMODATION LIMITED
INTENDING PASSENGERS MUST GIVE AT LEAST
SIXTEEN DAYS NOTICE

FOR FARES AND IMPORTANT NOTICES — SEE OVERLEAF

Above: Newhaven Town and King Arthur No. 799 *Sir Ironside* is on the down Continental Boat train on 28 August 1938. (Ernie's Railway Archive)

Right: Timetable showing the Newhaven boat train leaving at 4.14 p.m. This is the first one there had been since 6.09 a.m., but others soon followed at 4.27, 4.50, 5.14, 5.31 and 5.40 p.m., although three of these only ran when required. The 'EL' at the top of the column denoted a special schedule for an electric locomotive.

A man with a red flag had to walk in front of the train as it crossed the swing bridge leading to/from the west quay.

An A1X with a train of tankers and covered wagons leaves the west quay. The bridge was opened and closed by eight men turning a capstan.

The H2 4-4-2 Brighton Atlantics were best known for heading Newhaven boat trains. No. 32424 *Beachy Head* returned to Newhaven on an RCTS railtour on 13 April 1958.

Newhaven. The whole branch was built as a single track, but it was doubled in 1904. The first day of the service to Seaford was celebrated by giving passengers a free ride. Bunting was also displayed by ships in Newhaven Harbour, as well as from Bishopstone Tide Mills.

Before Southerham Junction is reached, however, the River Ouse had to be crossed. Although rarely used these days, there were riverside warehouses in Lewes that depended on river traffic as well as the Eastwood's Cement Works and Lewes Gasworks, both of which used the river to either receive fuel or raw materials or to transport their finished goods. This meant that the bridge could not be fixed. Little is known of the original bridge, but its replacement in 1893 consisted of five spans, with one being of the lifting bascule type. As rail and road traffic took the river traffic away, the need for a lifting bridge dwindled, and by the 1930s it was very rarely used.

After leaving the east coast line, the line follows the Ouse Valley. It passes through Southease and Rodmell Halt, which opened on 1 September 1906. There used to be a racecourse there from the late 1920s until the early 1940s, which would have brought some much-needed trade to the rural station.

The small town of Newhaven could boast three stations. The first one to be reached is Newhaven Town and, as its name suggests, serves the town rather than the port. Newhaven Harbour unsurprisingly was built to serve the harbour. The branch to Seaford diverges here, with the line carrying on to the third station, Newhaven Marine, which is where the boat trains terminated. It has only been called this since 1984, when British Railways changed it from Newhaven Harbour (Boat Station). Since 2006 it has not been open on safety grounds, due to the state of the roof. It has not been formally closed, however, and to comply with the law on parliamentary trains, one service calls there every day at 8 p.m., although this is not advertised. Services such as these are referred to as 'ghost trains'.

Newhaven was seen by the board of the LB&SCR as the port that would take over from Shoreham and be a rival to the SER's way to reach Paris. Although their Channel crossing from Dover was the shortest sea crossing, it meant that the rail journey was longer, making the London–Paris route via Newhaven overall the most direct route. The board wanted to run their own ferry services to Dieppe and formed the Brighton & Continental Steam Packet Company, but were prevented from doing so by legal difficulties preventing a railway company owning a steam packet company. Messrs Maples & Morris took over the running of the steamships but, in reality, it still remained part of the railway. In 1862 it was, however, granted powers to build and operate its own steamships and it went into partnership with the Western Railway of France, who supplied about two-thirds of the capital compared to the LB&SCR's one-third.

A London & Paris hotel was built in the 1870s, adjacent to the station, for continental travellers. It was requisitioned in the Second World War, being used both as offices and for accommodation. It never returned to its original use and was knocked down in the late 1960s.

In 1878 the Newhaven Harbour Co. was formed, which took over the running of the harbour from the harbour board. The numbers of passengers using the port to travel to France did not meet expectations and was only a fraction of the numbers using Dover or Folkestone. One of the problems was that the port was tidal and a regular service could not be run; departure times depended entirely on the tides. The LB&SCR tried to persuade the government to finance the rebuilding of the harbour but, when this strategy failed, they had no alternative but to finance it themselves. This work entailed filling in the Mill Creek so that the station could be moved southwards, and erecting a long concrete mole to the west of the mouth of the River Ouse. To help with the construction, a line was laid over the swing bridge running down the west bank of the Ouse.

Building the sea wall, which measures 2,800 feet, was a long and arduous task. A novel method of construction was used. A large chute was built near Sleeper's Hole. A lighter was moored beneath this, and cement and shingle was poured down the chute into large hessian bags in the lighter. These were then towed into position, and trap doors in the bottom of the hold were opened, allowing the bags to fall out and settle on the sea bed. Each bag weighed about 100 tons, and after six years the wall was only just over half completed. When it was finally completed in about 1879, the tracks were extended along the lower level of the mole.

A new harbour station was built in 1884 on reclaimed land, which meant that the platforms to Seaford had to be reached by a footbridge and walkway.

The First World War saw the closure of the port to passengers, but it became instrumental in supplying troops. Sidings were laid on the Down side of the tracks to park ammunition trains. Some ammunition was made locally at the South Heighton Cement Works, and this was brought to the sidings by the Newhaven Harbour Co. loco. One of the ammunition trains that was bringing supplies from further afield had a lucky escape when an Up goods had become divided in Redhill Tunnel on 18 April 1918. A following train ran into the loose wagons, derailing them. The ammunition train heading south ran into the derailed wagons. Although this train derailed, luckily it did not explode.

Electrification arrived in 1935, meaning a drastic cut in steam using the line. Boat trains from Newhaven Harbour continued to be in the hands of steam, with Brighton Atlantics often to be seen in charge. These were often ousted though by the three Southern Co-Co Electric locomotives, Nos 20001–3.

At Bishopstone, there used to be a large mill operated by the tide. At one time, this was the largest industrial building in Sussex. The main building was a four-storey granary with a windmill on the top. This mill was only used for raising and lowering bags of grain within the granary. It had been built in 1761 by the Duke of Newcastle but was taken over by William Catt. There was a small village on the site that housed the workers employed at the mill, and Bishopstone Beach station was opened to serve them. The name of the station was changed to Bishopstone Halt in 1922. The coming of the railway had not proved to be a blessing for the mill, as grain could be bought to the area by rail from other mills. By 1879, the Catt family had sold the mill, and the surrounding land and sea pounds, to the Newhaven Harbour Company, who used the premises as a bonded warehouse. There had also been a siding that went into the village, and this was worked by the Newhaven Harbour Company locomotive until the mill closed in 1900 and the line was lifted. The condition of the houses deteriorated over the years, and the village became uninhabitable in 1936, with any residents still there in 1939 being forcibly removed. The station closed in 1938 and a new Bishopstone station was built further to the east, opening in 1939.

The branch terminates at Seaford, which was reached in June 1864. It was designed as a through station as a railway had been proposed to extend the railway to Eastbourne, but the South Downs that lay between the two towns would have proved to be a formidable obstacle. The Eastbourne, Seaford & Newhaven Railway Co. was formed in 1886, but there was little enthusiasm for the venture and even the directors did not make it to a public meeting, blaming bad weather. The route was to have tunnelled under the South Downs to the Cuckmere Valley and then have headed north to Wilmington, where it would have joined the Lewes–Eastbourne line.

Heading eastwards from Southerham Junction, the first station to be reached is Glynde. The village is home to the world-famous opera house of Glyndebourne. Although the station is now a simple two-platform through station, it was once host to three industrial lines. Balcombe chalk pit was connected to the eastern end of the station, and there was a tramway from Brigden pit to the other end. There was also a clay pit that was connected to the station by the country's first telpherage line. This was an electric overhead wire railway, about a mile long, which was opened on 17 October 1885. The electricity needed to power the line was generated by a dynamo powered by a steam engine. It transported clay from a nearby pit and deposited it into trucks in the sidings. This clay was then taken to the Sussex Portland Cement Works at South Heighton. This overhead railway was replaced by a tramway in the late 1890s. All traces of these lines have disappeared.

Berwick comes next, opening in 1846 and extended in 1890. The signal box that controlled not only the signals but also the crossing gates was erected in 1879. It is a Saxby & Farmer Type 5 box that kept its original lever frame until the whole line became controlled by the operations centre at Three Bridges in 2015.

Polegate is now a shadow of its former self. The present station is the third one to be built in the village. When originally opened on 27 June 1846, it was sited where the

The Wealden Limited was an excursion run on 14 August 1955, having been postponed from 12 June due to a strike by ASLEF staff. Here L class 4-4-0 No. 31764 is in charge near Glynde.

(SOUTHERN)

EXCURSIONS
To BRIGHTON, WORTHING, EASTBOURNE, HASTINGS, ETC.
JUNE 11th to OCTOBER 31st, inclusive

SUNDAYS TO FRIDAYS
BY ANY TRAIN LEAVING AT OR BEFORE 11.0 a.m.

RETURN FARES, SECOND CLASS, TO:—

FROM	Brighton & Hove	Glynde-by-Sea	Lancing	Worthing Central	West Worthing	Lewes	Newhaven Town	Bishop- stone and Seaford	Eastbourne Pevensey Westham	Bexhill Central	St. Leonards (Warrior Square)	Hastings
MERSTHAM	7/-	7/3	8/3	8/3	8/9	6/9	8/6	9/3	11/3	11/3	11/3	11/3
GODSTONE	7/6	7/9	8/9	8/9	8/9	6/9	8/9	9/9	11/3	11/3	11/3	11/3
NUTFIELD	7/6	7/9	8/3	8/3	8/9	6/9	8/9	9/9	11/3	11/3	11/3	11/3
SHALFORD												
CHILWORTH & ALBURY }	9/9	10/9	11/3	11/9	13/-	9/9	11/-	11/6	12/9	14/3	14/6	14/—A
GOMSHALL & SHERE	9/-	10/-	10/6	11/-	11/6	8/9	10/3	10/9	12/-	13/6	13/9	14/3A
DORKING TOWN	8/-	9/-	9/6	10/-	10/3	7/9	9/3	9/6	11/-	13/-	13/-	13/-
DEEPDENE	8/-	9/-	9/6	10/-	10/3	7/9	9/3	9/6	11/-	13/-	13/-	13/-
BETCHWORTH	8/-	8/9	9/3	9/9	10/-	7/3	8/9	9/3	10/6	12/6	12/6	12/—A
REIGATE	6/9	7/9	8/3	8/9	8/9	6/6	8/-	8/3	9/9	11/3	11/6	11/9
REDHILL	8/-	7/3	8/3	8/3	8/9	6/6	7/6	8/3	9/9	10/9	11/3	11/3
EARLSWOOD	8/-	7/3	8/3	8/3	8/9	6/6	7/6	8/3	9/9	10/9	11/3	11/3
SALFORDS	8/-	6/9	7/3	7/9	8/-	6/-	7/-	8/-	9/9	10/3	10/6	10/6
HORLEY	8/-	6/9	7/3	7/6	7/6	5/3	6/6	7/-	8/9	10/3	10/6	10/6
GATWICK AIRPORT	8/-	6/-	6/9	7/-	7/-	4/3	6/3	4/9	8/9	10/3	10/3	10/—A

A—Fare to Hastings —3d. less.   B—For details of cheap tickets daily, see separate announcements.

EVERY SUNDAY, TUESDAY, WEDNESDAY & THURSDAY
Also on AUGUST BANK HOLIDAY
BY ANY TRAIN AFTER 11.0 a.m. TO 3.0 p.m. INCLUSIVE

RETURN FARES, SECOND CLASS, TO:—

FROM	Brighton and Hove	Shore- ham-by- sea	Lancing	Worthing Central and West Worthing	Lewes	New- haven Town	Bishop- stone and Seaford	East- bourne and Pevensey & Westham	Bexhill Central	St. Leonards (Warrior Square) and Hastings
MERSTHAM	4/9D	5/3	6/3	6/-	4/3	5/6	6/3	7/3	7/6	7/6
GODSTONE	4/3	5/9	6/3	4/6	4/9	5/6	6/9	7/6	7/6	7/6
NUTFIELD	4/9	4/3	5/9	4/-	4/9	5/6	5/9	7/6	7/6	7/6
SHALFORD										
CHILWORTH & ALBURY }	6/6	7/3	7/6	7/3	6/-	7/3	7/6	8/6	9/3	9/6
GOMSHALL & SHERE	6/3	7/-	7/3	7/6	6/-	7/-	7/3	8/3	8/9	8/9
DORKING TOWN	5/9	6/3	6/6	7/-	5/-	6/3	6/6	7/6	8/9	8/9
DEEPDENE	5/9	6/-	6/6	6/-	5/-	6/3	6/6	7/6	8/9	8/9
BETCHWORTH	5/3	5/9	6/-	6/3	5/-	5/9	6/-	7/3	8/3	8/3
REIGATE	4/9D	5/3	5/9	4/6	4/6	5/3	6/-	6/9	7/3	7/3
REDHILL	4/6D	5/-	5/6	4/6	4/6	5/3	5/9	6/9	7/3	7/6
EARLSWOOD	4/6D	4/9	5/6	5/3	4/6	4/6	5/3	6/9	7/3	7/3
SALFORDS	4/3D	4/9	5/-	5/3	4/-	5/-	5/3	6/3	6/9	6/9
HORLEY	3/9D	4/6	4/9	5/-	3/-	4/3	4/9	6/3	6/6	6/9
GATWICK AIRPORT	3/9D	4/3	4/6	4/9	3/-	4/3	4/3	6/3	6/3	6/—A

D—To Have only; for details of bookings daily to Brighton, see other side.

→ RETURN BY ANY TRAIN SAME DAY ←

Passengers should ascertain (if (and where) change of carriage is necessary

FIRST CLASS DAY EXCURSION TICKETS ARE ALSO OBTAINABLE
CHILDREN 3 AND UNDER 14 YEARS, HALF FARE
TICKETS MAY BE OBTAINED IN ADVANCE AT STATIONS OR AGENCIES

NOTICE AS TO CONDITIONS—These tickets are issued subject to the British Transport Commission's published Regulations and Conditions applicable to British Railways exhibited at their stations or obtainable free of charge at station booking offices.

Waterloo Station, S.E.1.
April, 1956

C.X.693/ A5 (D)
20044 (HO)

Printed in Great Britain by
Springer, Briggs, Stockley & Co., Kingston

Excursion leaflet from 1956, offering trips to Sussex resorts from London.

present-day station is now and was a simple through station between Lewes and Bexhill. To reach Eastbourne a horse-drawn bus had to be taken.

On 14 May 1849 it became a junction when east-facing junctions to Eastbourne and north to Hailsham were opened. These branches meant that the station was expanded to three through platforms and a bay. A single road engine shed was also constructed.

In 1881 a new, enlarged, second station was opened. This was sited away from the village as the branch to Hailsham was re-laid, leaving the station in a westward direction and allowing through trains from Eastbourne to be run without reversing. This meant relaying the curve eastwards, making it much tighter. Platforms were accessed via a subway from the larger station building. This subway also linked both sides of the village. This station building still survives and is used as a restaurant, which has many old railway photographs around the walls. The line to Hailsham had been extended in 1880 through Heathfield to Eridge and then to Tunbridge Wells. The new station had four through platforms and extensive sidings that in the 1960s were used to cut up redundant wagons as well as for the usual freight purposes.

The beginning of the end of this station was in 1965 when the line north of Hailsham was closed, and in 1968 the line to Hailsham was also closed. The original line that bypassed Eastbourne became little used with the reduction of freight services. Known locally as the 'loop line', it was closed in January 1969. It was double-tracked. The Up line was lifted on closure but the Down line was kept until 1974 and used as a mile-long engineer's siding. This was lifted in August 1984.

This station closed in 1986 when the present station was opened on the site of the original building. The closure of the second station caused much local controversy because the subway was also closed, meaning that the only way for pedestrians to go from one side of the track to the other was via the busy level crossing in the village centre.

The station once boasted three signal boxes. Polegate A controlled the junction to Hailsham and the goods yard; B controlled the junction to Eastbourne, and Polegate crossing controlled the crossing. This latter box still stands, thanks to resistance from local residents when the takeover of signalling from Three Bridges made the box redundant.

Taking the line to Eastbourne, it joins the line to Hastings at Willingdon Junction before entering Hampden Park station. This was opened in 1888 and was originally called Willingdon, being changed in 1903 to Willingdon for Hampden Park and eventually just Hampden Park. It did have a small goods yard but this closed in the 1960s. As it lies south of Willingdon Junction, it has one claim to fame in that it is the only station you pass through twice on the same journey. If you are travelling from Brighton to Hastings, for example, you pass through it once when approaching Eastbourne and then again when leaving. This means also that the level crossing is one of the busiest in the country, closing on average fourteen times every hour, causing major delays, especially in rush hours, as

Class E4 No. 32470 at Polegate station with two mineral wagons and a brake van making up the 3.05 p.m. goods service from Eastbourne on 16 May 1963. (Ernie's Railway Archive)

there are schools and a trading estate nearby. The signal box has just been demolished as part of the signalling upgrade, and has lost its semaphore signals, with everything now being controlled from Three Bridges.

Eastbourne was originally reached as a single-track branch from Polegate on 14 May 1849. There is an interesting chapter in a book called *East Bourne Memories* written by G. F. Chambers, who actually attended the opening ceremony. It lasted for fifteen hours and included a greasy pole being erected with a leg of mutton secured to the top, with the local youth being challenged to climb the pole, with the meat being the prize of any successful attempt. Festivities carried on into the evening with homemade fireworks being set off. He recalls the first train arriving in the town from Brighton around midday with dignitaries of the Brighton Company on board. They were treated to a luncheon in a large booth erected close to the station. The meal was followed by numerous speeches. Following the speeches the train was boarded again and a trip was made to Hailsham station, which also opened that day. All the return trips that day were pulled by the same engine, although another was standing by. The engine was driven by a man with the name of Jackson; the guard was a Mr Foster and the stationmaster was a Mr Dickinson. The station building resembled a simple wooden cottage but this was pulled down and replaced by a second building when Upperton Road was widened. This was again replaced in 1886 by the splendid building designed by F. D. Brick, which still stands.

In 1873 a line was built from just north of Willingdon, as it was then, to Pevensey, thus creating a triangle, giving lines both eastwards and westwards from Eastbourne as well as

The station name board says Hampden Park for Willingdon. It eventually became just Hampden Park. Class U1 No. 1902, introduced in 1928, heads into Eastbourne with a van and three coaches. Locals will also notice the absence of the concrete footbridge, which was built on the other side of the level crossing.

The station has been renamed and the pointwork has disappeared, as Class N No. 31866 stops on its way to Tunbridge Wells.

the original avoiding line. The opening of this line was celebrated at the Cavendish Hotel in Eastbourne, which was attended by directors of the company with invited local guests.

In 1877, the Duke of Devonshire instigated the building of a line by the SER from Ticehurst Road station into Eastbourne. The idea was to try to entice businessmen from the city to use the line, but there was no real interest in the idea and it was dropped.

In 1883 the first Municipal Mayor of Eastbourne, Mr Wallis, put forward a scheme for a more direct route from Eastbourne to the capital. The route would have been 48 miles long, leaving the LC&DR near Beckenham. It was to run via Edenbridge, Uckfield and Chiddingly, and cross the Brighton line just west of Polegate. The hearing into this line lasted eleven days and, although the people of Eastbourne gave their verbal support to it, financial support was less forthcoming, partly because the line did not serve any other large centres of population and would entail a lot of heavy engineering, with ten tunnels measuring nearly 7 miles between them.

In 1885 another scheme was put forward that would have linked Eastbourne with Seaford. Leaflets were distributed around Eastbourne extolling the virtues of the line, one of which was that it would mean cheaper coal, building materials and other goods, which were unloaded at Newhaven. The scheme was adopted by Parliament. The line would have turned left soon after leaving the present terminus, tunnelling under the South Downs with the eastern portal being near Rodmill Farm and exiting at East Dean. Another shorter tunnel would then be entered into before exiting at Seaford and joining the existing branch. Unfortunately there was a change of management at Brighton and the new manager Mr (to become Sir) Allen Sarle was against the idea and it was dropped.

This was not the last scheme to be brought forward as, in 1899, a light railway was planned, linking Pevensey to Robertsbridge. This was to be built to a 3-foot gauge, but it failed to attract much interest and was duly forgotten.

Mr Chambers travelled quite extensively and, while in Bournemouth in 1892, was impressed by the train services from other parts of the country, with carriages marked 'Through carriage to Bournemouth' arriving in the town belonging to London & North Western Railway, the Midland Railway and the Great Western. When he returned to Eastbourne, he wrote letters to the general managers of all the companies concerned, asking them to consider Eastbourne as a destination with trains travelling via Addison Road, Kensington and Clapham Junction. Although the LNWR agreed, Mr Sarle of the LB&SCR was totally opposed to the idea, stating that it would be unworkable due to the unpunctuality of the other company's trains. This was despite his own timetable having been described as 'a public scandal'. He was nothing if not tenacious, and letters to the press in the ensuing years finally brought success in 1904 when a through service from Manchester via Brighton was inaugurated, with the first train arriving on 23 July. The occasion was celebrated by a dinner at the Grand Hotel in Eastbourne, which was attended by directors of both companies. Although the service was initially to be only run through July, August and September, it was extended until the end of that year and then permanently through following years. His efforts to secure through services from the GWR were not successful, though.

While writing his book, Mr Chambers consulted his extensive diaries and one entry said that he went to Polegate on 5 July 1857 to meet his cousin returning from Croydon. When his train arrived it consisted of three engines, pulling fifty carriages. He was quite incredulous with his own entry but said it was written very clearly!

Eastbourne station had four platforms that had to be lengthened to cope with longer trains. There were two run-round loops between platforms 2 and 3 but, when the platforms were widened, this was reduced to one.

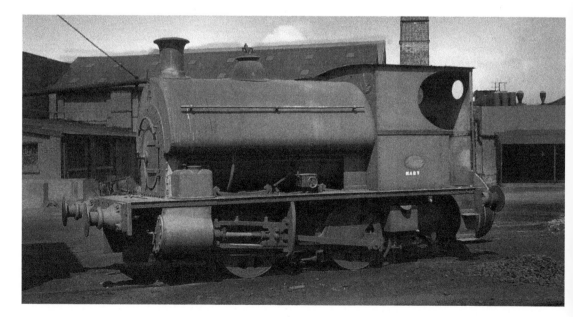

One of a pair of 0-4-0STs that worked in the gas works in Eastbourne until 1967. This one was named *Mary* – the other one was *Anne*.

A ring road was built in 1977 and Platform 4 had to be shortened to hold only eight coaches to make way for the road. This was taken out completely in 1991 during a re-signalling programme.

From 1849 the locomotives serving the station were originally stabled in a small shed, which was replaced by a roundhouse at the end of Platform 1 in 1876. This lasted until 1912 when a larger, seven-road shed was built about a mile outside the terminus. Hitler took a dislike to this and bombed it, causing extensive damage that was never repaired. It lost its status as a shed in 1952 but was used as a stabling centre for engines needed for services from Eastbourne as well as for storage for engines awaiting scrapping. What was left of the shed was demolished in 1969 and the site has remained as wasteland.

Right: Edwardian days at Eastbourne with two lady trainspotters?! The roundhouse can be seen on the left. The signal box on the right and the houses behind it are the only survivors from this scene.

Below: The LB&SCR used to use the Crumbles line to photograph their latest stock as there was nothing in the background to distract from the train. Here Marsh Class I2 4-4-2T No. 19 poses with a seven-car Pullman train.

Inside the roundhouse at Eastbourne are two decorated locomotives that have been used on the annual trip organised by the Station Masters' and Inspectors' Mutual Aid Fund – the loco on the left has come from Victoria and the one on the right from London Bridge.

E4 tank No. 32515 shunts the coal yard at Eastbourne on 17 July 1955. This site is now a car dealership and builder supplier's site.

The 'Wealdsman' railtour, having arrived in Eastbourne from Three Bridges in the hands of N class No. 31411 and U class No. 31803. The tour stayed in town for about an hour before the pair of locos departed for Haywards Heath. The centre track was once a release road and run-round loop for engines, but was by then just used for storage.

A photographer curses the railings at Eastbourne shed as he photographs N15 King Arthur class
No. 796 *Sir Dodinas le Savage.*

There was an extensive goods yard adjacent to Platform 1, with a large, typically
LB&SCR-designed goods shed. The goods shed still survives as the Enterprise shopping
centre while the rest of the goods yard is now a car park. When leaving Eastbourne there
was a large coal yard on the right, between Cavendish Place and Whitley Road Bridges.
This is now occupied by a car dealership and yard of a builder's merchants.

The station was signalled by a superb box with a 108-lever frame built in 1882. This
lever frame was replaced by a smaller seventy-two-lever frame in 1934. This frame was
made redundant in 1991 when colour light signals were installed and the points became
power operated. The whole box has now been made redundant, as the station is now
controlled centrally from Three Bridges. Both the station buildings and signal box are
now safeguarded as they are both listed buildings.

A branch was built in 1862 that left the line from just north of the station and
finished on an area of land known as The Crumbles. This is a large area of shingle that
the LB&SCR used for ballast on their tracks. It was also used by the LB&SCR when
they wished to photograph their new trains, as there was nothing in the background
to distract from their latest stock. A spur was added when a new gasworks was built in
1870. In 1926 another spur was constructed from this line to serve the Corporation's
Electric Light depot at Roselands. This line was built to deliver coal for the boilers. The
bus company that had a depot opposite in Churchdale Road also had their fuel delivered
by rail for a time. The line closed in 1967.

On 25 August 1958 there was a serious accident when an overnight sleeper train from
Glasgow collided with a twelve-coach commuter train leaving for London, pushing it
back into the buffers. The accident was caused by the incoming train overrunning a red
signal. Four passengers and the motorman were killed by the 25-mph impact. Twenty-two
were injured, five of them seriously.

Leaving Eastbourne in an easterly direction towards Hastings, you joined the direct line from Polegate after passing Hampden Park again and taking the right-hand track at Willingdon Junction; you would then reach Pevensey and Westham station, which opened in 1851, followed by Pevensey Bay, which opened in September 1905 as Pevensey Bay Halt. It kept this name until May 1969. Next is Normans Bay, which opened on the same day as Pevensey Bay Halt. It was originally named Pevensey Sluice before being called Normans Bay Halt. The halt status was also removed on the same day as that of Pevensey Bay. Local legend has it that it was only built because a whale was washed ashore, causing hordes of Londoners to flock to the area; a station was hastily built to accommodate them. There is very little else there to warrant a station.

Two railway staff at a desolate Normans Bay watch a 4-4-0 storm past with a three-car birdcage set.

A D class tank enters Cooden with a Hastings–Brighton direct train that missed out Eastbourne. The station nameplate places the date between 1922 and 1935.

Cooden Beach station was opened on 11 September 1905 as Cooden Golf Halt. It changed to Cooden Halt by 1922 and then again to Cooden Beach in 1935. Collington, the next station along the line, is another small two-platform station that opened in 1905 as Collington Wood Halt. It closed a year later, and then reopened as Bexhill West Halt, before becoming Collington Halt in 1929. The halt was dropped in 1969.

Bexhill comes next and is a somewhat larger station. When it opened on 27 June 1846 it was known as Bexhill Central. The town had another station, Bexhill West, which is described in the chapter on the main line to Hastings.

It could at one time boast the longest platforms outside of London. This is because in 1911 it was lengthened to accommodate the funeral train of Nripendra Narayan, the Maharaja of Cooch Behar. He had come to Bexhill to convalesce after an illness, but died in the town on 11 September 1911. He was buried eleven days later, so the company had less than a fortnight to lengthen the platforms – it could never happen these days!

The station buildings have now been given listed status.

At Glyne Gap, the Hastings & St Leonards Gas Company had their works. The gas works opened in 1904 and was in full production by 1907. The site included three sidings, which were accessed from a westerly direction. Natural gas saw the end of production in 1986. It was at the end of De La Warr Road and the site has now been covered by the Ravenside Retail Park. There was also a station there called Glyne Gap Halt. It was very short-lived, opening in 1905 and closing ten years later.

Most of the stations on the line between Eastbourne and Hastings are still operational; however, one that does not exist anymore is St Leonards West Marina. It was opened on 7 November 1846 by the Brighton, Lewes & Hastings Railway. The original terminus was a temporary one at Bulverhythe in June of that year. When the River Asten had been crossed, the new terminus further east was reached. This was originally called Hastings & St Leonards. An engine shed, sidings and freight facilities were also built there. The shed, which also boasted a turntable, was responsible for supplying engines for services to London. It was originally a two-road shed but, in 1872, a new four-road shed was built, which was enlarged again in 1898 and by BR in 1949. Many of the famous Schools Class of loco were shedded there when they were responsible for the Hastings–London expresses. Electrification of the South Coast lines robbed the shed of much of its importance, as did dieselisation of the line to London. Allocation to the shed (74E) dwindled and in 1958 the shed closed, although it stayed open as a stabling point. The shed was demolished in 1976 and a train washing plant now covers the site.

Bo Peep Tunnel lies between West Marina and Warrior Square. It is 1,318 yards long.

Hastings was on the eastern border of LB&SCR territory and a feud with its rival, the SER, ensued over routes and stations. The SER had built a station at Warrior Square, but LB&SCR trains were not allowed to call there until 1870. The LB&SCR then changed the name of Hastings & St Leonards to St Leonards West Marina. Warrior Square was in a more convenient location, but West Marina did survive, even becoming the terminus for London trains in 1949 when Bo Peep Tunnel had to be closed for repairs. It finally closed for passenger traffic in July 1967; this took place about five years after goods services had been withdrawn.

Before the Brighton, Lewes & Hastings Railway had been taken over by the LB&SCR, a deal had been done to build a line linking up with the SER at Ashford. This route would have linked Brighton with Dover, which was of strategic military importance to the country. The SER wanted to protect its territory, and so it did a deal with the government that they would build the Hastings–Ashford line in return for powers allowing them to build the North Kent line. The BLH railway agreed to let the SER go ahead with this scheme in return for running powers over their lines into Hastings. However, the SER made life very difficult for the LB&SCR run into Hastings by holding up their trains so long at Bo Peep tunnel that they returned to St Leonards to unload their passengers. The SER even went so far as tearing up tracks and blocking the line with wagons to disrupt the LB&SCR trains. The disruption was brought to a halt when the LB&SCR won an injunction against its rival. An agreement was finally reached when the two companies agreed to share revenues created by the line.

The Oxted Lines

We've explored the four lines that still serve Lewes, but there was another one that was not built for the primary purpose of making money, but rather for keeping out rival companies. The Lewes & Uckfield Railway was authorised to build a railway between the two towns in 1857. The line was a relatively easy one to build as it followed the courses of the River Ouse and River Uck. The line opened the following year on 11 October to much celebration and merriment. The Maiden's Head Inn hosted a dinner for 100 invited guests, while those without tickets enjoyed a firework display, bands and a procession.

The first train to arrive at Lewes consisted of two locomotives hauling sixteen carriages full of excited passengers. In 1864 the line became part of the LB&SCR's growing empire. The new owners sought a better entrance into Lewes that would avoid the tunnel; a new junction was built immediately to the east of the station and the line left the town via a

Class E4 No. 32582 is about to hand over the single-line token southbound at Culver Junction on 2 September 1953 with an Oxted–Brighton train.

bridge over the High Street linking up with the existing track near Hamsey. This meant that trains from Brighton could access the line without reversing. The original earthworks are still visible from the train south of Cooksbridge.

After leaving the town of Lewes, before the first country station was reached the line divided at Culver Junction, with the left-hand line heading towards East Grinstead via the Bluebell line and the right-hand line heading through Uckfield and Eridge. The village of Barcombe is situated just after the junction and had a station on both branches. Barcombe, which had to wait eighteen years for a station, opened in 1882. It was originally New Barcombe to distinguish itself from Barcombe Mills, but the 'New' was dropped at the start of 1885. Rather confusingly, Barcombe Mills had just been called Barcombe but became Barcombe Mills on the day New Barcombe became Barcombe!

Newick and Chailey had impressive station buildings, which even included a restaurant, that belied its country location between the two villages it served. The two platforms formed a passing loop on the single-track line. The buildings on the Up side were demolished in the 1930s. It opened on 1 August 1882. The closure of the line was a long, drawn-out affair that has been well documented. It originally closed on 29 May 1955, but was forced to reopen on 5 August 1956, mainly due to the efforts of a Miss Bessemer of Chailey, who found in the Act of Parliament that authorised the line a clause that imposed an obligation on British Railways to continue running trains. Another Act of Parliament was needed to repeal this. It finally closed on 17 March 1958.

LB&SCR 4-4-0 Class B4 No. 42, named *His Majesty*, nears Barcombe Mills. The engine was to lose its name in Southern days and was withdrawn in April 1947 after giving about forty-five years of service.

A very rural Balcombe station was the setting for this photo of LB&SCR Class B1 0-4-2 No. 185 *George A. Wallis*, built as early as July 1889. The class were commonly referred to as 'Gladstones'. It was withdrawn in early 1923.

On 30 April 1955, an ex-LMS 4P 2-6-4T loco, No. 42081, calls at Barcombe station on an Oxted–Brighton via East Grinstead and Lewes service.

No. 80033, a Std Class 4, calls at Newick & Chailey on 28 May 1955 on a Brighton–Victoria via Lewes, East Grinstead and Oxted service.

Class C2X No. 32442 leaves Cinderhill Tunnel with an East Grinstead–Brighton service.

Sheffield Park was the next station up the line, which is now the headquarters of the preserved Bluebell Railway. The two years' stay of execution on the line gave the Bluebell Preservation Society precious time to organise themselves. The society has honoured the efforts of Miss Bessemer by naming the restaurant and bar 'The Bessemer Arms'.

Sheffield Park station opened in August 1882 as part of Lewes & East Grinstead Railway, which had been authorised in 1877. It was built on land owned by the Earl of Sheffield, at his request. When opened, it was called Fletching and Sheffield Park, but the Fletching was dropped after the Earl objected to it.

Horsted Keynes, the next station up the line, was the junction of a branch that left the main Brighton line just north of Haywards Heath and also served Ardingly. This line created a secondary route to London from the South Coast. Because of this, its survival was ensured for a few more years. The line was also electrified in 1935 and a service from Seaford terminated there. For about a year the station was served by both British Railways and the Bluebell Railway before British Railways withdrew its services in 1963.

West Hoathly was one of the stations on this line and the Polegate–Tunbridge Wells Cuckoo Line that was built in a large country house style. They have been described as being in the 'Domestic Revival' style, costing around £17,000 each to build, which was a not insubstantial sum for a station that had no large centre of population in the surrounding area. They were designed to appeal to those Londoners who were looking to move to the area and use the stations for commuting purposes.

The station could boast a five-road goods yard with a cattle dock and small wooden goods shed. There was even a railway hotel opposite the station that became a public house on the closure of the railway; it is now a private house.

Class U1 No. 31902 slows for Ardingly on 28 May 1955 with a Brighton–Victoria via Oxted train.

The Wealden Limited was a railtour operated by the RCTS on 14 August 1955. Class H2 No. 32426 *St. Albans Head* was photographed heading north at Horsted Keynes.

No. 41302, an Ivatt ex-LMS 2-6-2T, is at Horsted Keynes on 28 May 1955. An electric unit waits in the adjoining platform with a service to Seaford. That was the only platform that had a third rail.

The station closed with the line in 1955 but, like others on the line, was forced to reopen. The station buildings had all been demolished by the end of 1967, but the proposed housing estate was never built; the Bluebell Railway now own the site and plan to rebuild the station.

Kingscote station was opened in 1882. Its station buildings and canopies were built on a fairly grand scale, bearing in mind that there were very few residential properties nearby. It has the dubious honour of being one of the least used stations on the Southern Railway. It was closed in 1955 with the other stations on the line, but was not reopened when others were forced to because it was not mentioned in the original Act.

It has now been reopened by the Bluebell Railway.

East Grinstead was the only town with any significant population on the line, which has ensured its survival on a line from London. It opened in August 1882 and has undergone many changes. The station was built on two levels, with the Lewes line passing underneath the line from Three Bridges to Tunbridge Wells. This upper level closed in 1967.

When the line from Lewes opened in 1882, East Grinstead was the northern terminus of the line until 10 March 1884 when the Croydon, Oxted & East Grinstead Railway opened. This made through running to the capital achievable, with four through trains from Brighton being run every day, with London Bridge being used as the northern terminus. Although this was a shorter route between the two terminii, the route via Haywards Heath and Three Bridges was the faster.

On a service to Victoria from Brighton, ex-LMS 4P No. 42105 approaches Kingscote on 28 May 1955.

Oxted station with H class No. 31308 waiting to leave for Tunbridge Wells West. (Edwin Wilmshurst)

The station buildings were substantial, with a restaurant and even a billiards room that were only available to rail passengers.

A small engine shed was built there, with a D1 tank allocated to it to operate the first train in the morning. It only lasted until 1894 when Three Bridges and Tunbridge Wells West were responsible for supplying the motive power over the line.

When the line to Lewes closed in 1958, few trains used the lower level, with passengers for London travelling from the high level via Three Bridges. Six years later, some trains via Oxted were timetabled to finish at the low-level station and in 1967, when the Three Bridges to Tunbridge Wells line closed, all London-bound trains started from there.

The old station buildings were demolished, as was the bridge over the London Road, although some of the abutments still survive. The line was electrified in 1987 and a new station building was erected. The Bluebell Railway reached East Grinstead from Horsted Keynes in March 2013 and a steam service ran from London again when *Tornado* visited in July 2014.

Leaving East Grinstead to the north, the line crosses the county border into Surrey.

The Lewes & Uckfield Railway was given authority in 1856 to build a line between the two towns. They had been encouraged to build the line following the opening of the line from Brighton. It opened in 1858 but, within a year, it had been taken over by the LB&SCR. Another company, the Brighton, Uckfield & Tunbridge Wells company, was incorporated to extend the line. The 12-mile section ran from Uckfield to a junction at Groombridge with the East Grinstead–Tunbridge Wells line. This line was also taken over by the LB&SCR before it opened.

If we return to Culver Junction and take the right-hand route, we pass through Barcombe Mills and then reach Isfield. It was opened in October 1858 and closed in May 1969. In 1983 the station and a short length of track bed were purchased by the Milham family, who owned a gardening firm; they had plans to restore the buildings and open a short length of track. The family sold up in 1990 and the site is now the headquarters of the Lavender Line, a small preservation railway named after a local coal merchant who operated from the goods yard.

Traffic on the line started to decline in the 1960s and it became one of Beeching's cuts, although not without a fight from local residents and 'dirty tricks' from British Railways. New timetables were introduced, meaning long waits for connections. The original aim was to close the whole line between Hurst Green Junction and Lewes. The objections were partially successful, with only the section south of Uckfield being lost. BR had claimed that the bridge over the River Ouse was unsafe on one side and so a shuttle service was introduced. This shuttle service did not meet with trains leaving Uckfield, so more

Uckfield signal box and crossing gates, which used to hold up traffic using the High Street, on 13 January 1962. N class No. 31870 approaches on a passenger service from Tonbridge. The current station has been moved to the other side of the road and the gates have long since gone. (Edwin Wilmshurst)

passenger traffic was lost. Engineers then pronounced that the bridge was completely unsafe and all rail traffic was stopped. BR then introduced a bus service – but the lane was not wide enough for buses to reach Barcombe Mills station, so a taxi was provided to take passengers to the bus stop!

Uckfield station became a terminus when the line to Lewes was closed in 1969. For trains to reach the station, the main road through the town had to be crossed via a level crossing. This situation was alleviated by building a new station on the other side of the road; the original station was demolished along with the goods shed in 2000 after they had been damaged by floodwater. The signal box still survives but is now used as an office for a taxi company.

The line north of Uckfield was singled in 1990 when the tracks to the south closed. Leaving Uckfield, the next station up the line is Buxted, which opened in 1868, followed by Crowborough. This opened in the same year, originally as Rotherfield. In 1881, it was renamed Crowborough station and subsequently Crowborough & Jarvis Brook. In 1974 it reverted to Crowborough.

The line from Heathfield and Hailsham is joined before Eridge is reached. This used to be an important station, with three lines joining there. The aforementioned line, from Heathfield to the south, carried on north before leaving at Birchden Junction for Tunbridge Wells West. When the remaining line was singled, only the Up line was needed and the Down line, platform and buildings were abandoned. The Spa Valley Railway have taken advantage of this and have gradually expanded their operations from Tunbridge Wells West; they now use the restored facilities at Eridge so that their customers can reach the preservation line by rail.

Class U1 No. 31909 arrives at Ashurst with an Oxted–Brighton via Lewes service.

12 June 1962 saw H class No. 31005 near Ashurst with a two-coach passenger train.

H class No. 31544 crosses the River Medway just outside Ashurst on 12 June 1962.

Std 4 No. 80037 on a Victoria–Brighton service passes U1 No. 31909 at Ashurst on 12 June 1962. The train has divided, and the U1 will reverse on to the remaining portion and take them on to Groombridge and Tunbridge Wells West.

London-bound trains carry on their journey via Ashurst on the Surrey/Sussex border and Cowden to Croydon and London.

Cuckoo Line

The last of the LB&SCR lines to journey along was the Cuckoo Line between Polegate and Tunbridge Wells. The first section to open was on 14 May 1849 – the same day as the then branch from Polegate to Eastbourne opened. The line took its name from the Cuckoo Fair that was held in Heathfield in April. Celebrations were held to mark the opening, with dignitaries arriving in the afternoon after they had visited Eastbourne. A band played while the local youth tucked into roast beef and plum pudding.

Hailsham served one of the larger centres of population along the line and had the facilities to match. The Cuckoo Line was single-track for its entire length and, when the line opened, Hailsham only had one platform. When the line was extended north, it became a passing place with another platform. However it had to wait over thirty years for this to happen. The station also had a fairly large goods yard with a goods shed. There was also a single-road engine shed adjacent to the platform, but this went when the line was extended. Materials from the shed were used to build a new stationmaster's house. Hailsham has long been a market town and still holds weekly cattle auctions not far from the station, which had facilities to handle livestock.

The station building differed from others on the line, not being built in the country house style, but being single-storey with a gable at either end.

The goods shed at Hailsham abutted the Up platform and was built in typical LB&SCR style. Std Class 4 tank No. 80032 enters with a northbound train on its way to Tunbridge Wells.

Right: Posing by Hailsham's signal box was K class No. 32351, on an unknown date.

Below: Battle of Britain No. 34066 *Spitfire* heads the 'Sussex Downsman' RCTS LCGB tour south through Hailsham on 22 March 1964.

Std Class 4 2-6-4T No. 80068 heads north through Hailsham, *circa* 1960.

The next station up the line was Hellingly, which opened in 1880 as a single platform alongside the single track. Ten years later, two sidings had been added. It would have remained just another quiet wayside station, if it were not for the fact that a large lunatic asylum was built just outside the village, served by its own railway. It was initially built by the contractors to supply materials for constructing the large complex of buildings and was steam-operated. When the hospital was completed in 1905, the railway was taken over by East Sussex County Council, who decided to electrify it using overhead wires to transport patients, visitors and goods to and from the hospital. A separate platform was constructed for the hospital services, as well as sidings for the transfer of goods between railways. The hospital's passenger service ended in 1931, but the line stayed open to carry coal to feed the hospital's boilers. In 1959 they switched to fuel oil, causing the line to close and the track to be lifted. Any trace of the line soon disappeared apart from a building that was used as a shed for the locos, which was taken over by a motor mechanic, still housing much of the electrical equipment on the end wall as late as the 1980s. The whole hospital, which had a terrible reputation locally, was closed in 1994; there is now a large housing estate called Roebuck Park covering the site.

Continuing our northward journey, the next station was Horam, which has had a few name changes over the years. When the line opened in 1880 it was named Horeham Road for Waldron, a name that it kept until 1890, when it became Horeham Road and Waldron. In 1900 it became Waldron and Horeham Road, which lasted until 1935 when it was simplified to Waldron and Horam. In 1953 it underwent its final change when it became just Horam. Although the station buildings have been demolished, there is a very short length of platform that still survives just under the road bridge, and the locals have restored this and replaced the Horam running-in sign as well as erecting some platform

Overhead electric railway at Hellingly on 5 May 1956. (Edwin Wilmshurst)

Horam station saw BR Std 4 2-6-4T No. 80032 heading south towards Eastbourne on 4 June 1965. (Keith Harwood)

fencing. Much of the trackbed between Polegate and Heathfield now forms the Cuckoo Trail, which is a cycle path and footpath. In its heyday the station could only boast of three sidings. Much of the freight traffic was milk, as Express Dairies had a depot there with farmers bringing milk to the station in churns. From there it was transferred to tankers that left the station at 8.20 p.m. every night, bound for Eastbourne.

Heathfield was a market town and reached after a long 1-in-50 climb from Hellingly. It was one of the larger stations on the route, about on a par with Hailsham. It had a six-road goods yard that included a goods shed, end loading bay and cattle dock. It also had a water tank to replenish locomotives. This was fed by a borehole 370 feet deep, but this had a tendency to run dry during long spells without rain. In 1896 a decision was taken to deepen the bore hole and it was while this was being done that natural gas was found. This was harnessed and stored on site, and was used to light the station. It was also used to drive a pump to bring water from the well to the water tank. The station buildings were on an overbridge with platforms reached by stairs. The station building still exists and is now a shop selling kitchen wares.

Immediately to the north of the station is a 266-yard tunnel through which the line continues to climb, reaching a summit of just under 500 feet before Mayfield is reached. The tunnel was built wide enough to accommodate twin tracks, and two tracks were laid through its entire length, although one of them was a headshunt for the goods yard. Mayfield also had a four-road goods yard and shed. Unlike the stations to the south, this

A light load for Std 4 2-6-4T No. 80085 as it heads north through Mayfield in 1962. (Keith Harwood)

This is another completely unrecognisable location now. A BR Std 4 tank leaves Mayfield, heading south. The bridge and parapets have completely disappeared. (Edwin Wilmshurst)

yard could only be directly accessed from the north, so northbound freights had to use the headshunt and then set back into the yard.

The area that used to be the goods yard has now disappeared under the Mayfield bypass, which is in a deep cutting. The station building still exists as a private dwelling but the recent tenant has let it fall into a state of disrepair. It recently came on to the market for around £330,000 and the new owner has started to restore it.

After passing through a short tunnel that takes the line under the A267, Rotherfield and Mark Cross is reached. It lies in a valley between the two villages. Any passengers arriving at the station faced a stiff climb to either of the two villages. Like Mayfield, it was built in LB&SCR's country house style and is now a residential property. The station boasted two platforms and a passing loop. The new owner had the novel idea of using the trackbed between the platforms to create an outside swimming pool. Like Mayfield, the four-road goods yard was only accessed directly from the north.

After leaving Rotherfield and Mark Cross, the line met up with the line from Lewes at Redgate Mill Junction before entering Eridge. The two lines initially were both operated as single tracks running parallel with each other for over a mile and a quarter but, when the line to Uckfield was doubled in 1894, a junction was installed and the two tracks became Up and Down lines.

The Cuckoo Line closed for passenger traffic north of Hailsham in 1965, but the section between Polegate and Heathfield remained open for freight. A lorry hit a bridge just north of Hailsham in April 1968 and it was deemed uneconomical to repair as it was

There may not be a train in sight, but there are plenty of interesting items on the platforms of Rotherfield & Mark Cross. (Ian D Nolan)

already earmarked for closure. Passenger traffic to Hailsham lingered on until September 1968 with diesel multiple units operating services, after which the whole line closed.

It is worth noting that a book was published in 1910 by G. F. Chambers of Eastbourne, who wrote a chapter on the railways of Eastbourne. Mr Chambers, who was both a barrister and a JP, was not overly enamoured with the service or comfort offered by the Brighton company. He states that the carriages were inferior to those operated by 'the great Northern companies'. Before 1865 there were four classes, with the fourth having open sides but also a roof. He also states that there was great excitement when Second Class carriages were introduced with leather seats and a narrow leather cushion for a backrest.

In 1864, Mr Chambers was shown a letter from the London solicitors Currey & Holland, advisors to the Duke of Devonshire, who owned large parts of Eastbourne. It stated that the South Eastern Railway wanted to encroach on LB&SCR territory and proposed building a branch from Battle. A meeting was subsequently held in the Burlington Hotel, Eastbourne, with the SER's engineer, Mr F. Brady, and Mr H. Toogood, to discuss the project. Plans had been drawn up that showed the line was to be 13.5 miles long with a new terminus at the back of Terminus Road, near Tideswell Road. It was reported that the line was never built because the Brighton Company 'squared' their rivals and the project was withdrawn. This was achieved by an agreement that, if the SER agreed not to build this line, they would be allowed to run two return trips per day over a proposed line from Tunbridge Wells to Eastbourne.

The Ouse Valley line, together with the Surrey and Sussex lines, were started but the financial crash of 1866 put a stop to work on the lines, and eventually Parliament sanctioned their abandonment. Although some lines were put to Parliament again and assent was given, some lines were never revived, although the original earthworks still exist – between Balcombe and Uckfield, for example. The original line between Groombridge and Hailsham included a long tunnel under Heathfield, but would have lent itself to much faster services than the revised Cuckoo Line did. This first project was abandoned by the LB&SCR in 1864. In 1873, local businessmen promoted a cheaper 3-foot gauge line with steep gradients and tight curves and got parliamentary approval to build the line; however, they found they could not raise the necessary capital to construct it. They consequently offered it to the LB&SCR, who turned down the offer. The promoters then threatened to offer it to the SER, which spurred the LB&SCR into action; they took over the route but altered it to ease the curves and gradients. The first section was opened between Hailsham and Heathfield in 1880.

Railway history may have had to be rewritten if a plan to unite the LB&SCR with the SER and the LC&DR had gone ahead. The merger gained parliamentary approval in the Commons but when it was heard in the Lords, Lord Redesdale insisted that the SER, whose fares were much higher than those of the other two companies, lowered theirs to a comparative level. They refused to do this, so the amalgamation never went ahead.

The 'Brighton's' attitude to their rivals was shown by the general manager at the time, Mr J. P. Knight, at a meeting in his office with G. F. Chambers. He pulled out a map of Sussex and marked out with a pencil all the existing and proposed lines. He then said with a chuckle, 'Look at this. Isn't this a defensive strategy worthy of the Duke of Wellington?'

Another line that was proposed and built by the LB&SCR was the Lewes & East Grinstead Line in 1877, which was to extend to join the Surrey & Sussex Line at Oxted.

In the previous year, plans had been put forward by the LC&DR for a Beckenham, Lewes & Brighton Railway. This was fiercely rejected by the LB&SCR and the plans were defeated, but the scheme was revived again in 1864 with branches to Westerham and Eastbourne. It was to follow a route through West Wickham, Oxted, East Grinstead, Newick, Lewes and Rotingdean. It was contested and thrown out again, but it did stir the Brighton company into realising they had to defend their territory by building more lines in East Sussex. Later that year, various Bills were obtained including the Ouse Valley line through Balcombe to Uckfield, the St Leonards line from Hailsham to Hastings, and the

Tunbridge Wells and Eastbourne line via Groombridge and Heathfield. The latter was to become a main line if Parliament sanctioned the 'Surrey and Sussex' project, which would have run from Croydon through Edenbridge and Groombridge to Tunbridge Wells. These Bills received Parliamentary Assent but a Mr Curtis of Windmill Hill objected to the St Leonards section, meaning it had to wait until the following year when revised plans were accepted. The Surrey and Sussex scheme was taken over by the LB&SCR.

The LB&SCR was very active in defending its territory and blocked many proposed schemes that would have improved services to Brighton. It also built lines, not so much for profit, but to keep rival companies out of what it regarded as its territory.

SER Routes

Up until now, all the routes we have looked at were operated by the LB&SCR, many of which were built to keep out rival companies. They were not completely successful in their attempts, as the South Eastern Railway (SER) reigned supreme in the east of the county.

   The first railway to reach Hastings was the LB&SCR with their route from Lewes. This was in 1846 with a terminus station near St Leonards. Five years later Hastings was reached from the other direction by the SER with a line from Ashford. In order to link up with the LB&SCR and their own line from Tonbridge via Battle, the SER had to build two tunnels: the Hastings tunnel and Bo Peep tunnel. A station, St Leonards Warrior Square, was built in the small area between the two tunnels. Services started in February 1851 but the two companies did not cooperate with each other, as has been described previously in this book, with loaded trucks being left to block trains and track being

St Leonards Warrior Square in Southern days.

pulled up. The arguments were settled by court action and an agreement was reached wherein receipts were shared. Each railway had its own platform at Hastings – a terminal one for LB&SCR services and a through platform for the SER.

In 1899, the SER merged with the London, Chatham & Dover Railway (L&CDR) to form the South Eastern & Chatham Railway (SE&CR).

In 1931 Hastings station was rebuilt, with all platforms being through lines and with the buildings being reconstructed in a Neo-Georgian style.

Leaving Hastings for London, the line heads west through the 788-yard Hastings tunnel to St Leonards Warrior Square. It was opened by the SER in 1851 and called Gensing. Under the agreement with LB&SCR, their trains were not allowed to stop there. This arrangement lasted until 1870. Upon leaving Warrior Square another tunnel is encountered – the 1,318-yard Bo Peep tunnel. This has been a constant source of trouble due to leakage from underground springs. Although the track through it was double, it had to be singled in 1885 due to reduced clearance. It was rebuilt in 1906 to allow the doubling of the tracks again.

There used to be another station at St Leonards and this was West Marina. This was the first station in the area to open in 1846, when it was called Hastings & St Leonards. When the tunnel had been built and the line extended to Hastings, its name was changed simply to St Leonards and then to West Marina in 1870. It was enlarged over the years to include sidings, a goods yard with shed and an engine shed with turntable, coaling and watering facilities. The station closed in 1967 and the area it covered is now taken up by carriage-washing facilities.

The track divides at Bo Peep Junction with the LB&SCR line heading west, while the SER lines turn northwards. Another station is arrived at immediately after the junction. This is West St Leonards. It was built by the SER in 1887 as competition for the LB&SCR's West Marina station.

The next station up the line is Crowhurst, although it did not open until 1902, a full fifty years after the line opened. A branch had been built from the station that went over a seventeen-arch viaduct to a new terminus at Bexhill, called Bexhill West. Seven contractors' steam locos were used in the construction of the line. Crowhurst station was very spacious, with Up and Down through platforms and two bay platforms – one either side of the main line. The branch was built by the Crowhurst, Sidley & Bexhill Railway, but was operated by the SER. It was built because residents of Bexhill or those choosing to visit the resort had to use LB&SCR trains, either by travelling via Eastbourne or via Hastings after changing from the London service.

On leaving Crowhurst, the Coombe Valley had to be crossed; this was achieved by the seventeen-arch viaduct measuring 416 yards in length and 67 feet in height, and using approximately 9 million bricks. It was known also known as the Crowhurst or Sidley viaduct. It took two years to build due to the land it was built on being marshland, meaning it needed concrete foundations measuring up to 32 feet deep.

Sidley was the only intermediate station on the route. This was set in a cutting and had its own three-road goods yard and shed. Predictions of the freight to be handled at the station proved to be overly optimistic and the goods shed was sold in 1929 to a local builder's merchant. It survived until 2009, when it was demolished to make way for new industrial units. The station buildings were at street level, with passengers having to descend to the platforms via a flight of steps. The line was temporarily closed in 1917 with the footbridge and track being taken to France to help with the war effort. It reopened in June 1920.

The line, which was double tracked throughout, then entered the splendid terminus at Bexhill West. This was another station that was renamed several times. It opened as Bexhill, becoming Bexhill-on-Sea in 1920. This name only lasted three years before it became Bexhill Eastern in July 1923, and finally Bexhill West in November 1929. Its size indicates the expectations the builders had for the line, which sadly never materialised.

There were three platforms, two of which had a 400-foot glass canopy over their 700-foot length. The station received an unexpected upturn in trade in 1949 when Bo Peep tunnel had to be closed for repairs, with the result that all trains that usually served Hastings were diverted to Bexhill West.

It also boasted a large goods yard, four carriage sidings, two signal boxes and a two-road engine shed. Goods traffic also never achieved the amount of trade that had been hoped for, and towards the end the sidings were used for storage of redundant stock.

When the coastal route was electrified in the 1930s, passenger traffic fell. Push-pull services were introduced, with H classes in charge of trains to and from Crowhurst. Through services to London were withdrawn at the start of the Second World War and were never reinstated. Goods traffic consisted of a daily freight train to Tonbridge but this ended on 1 September 1963 with passenger traffic ending the following year. The track was lifted and platforms demolished. The wonderful station buildings were thankfully spared, however, and have had various purposes since, including being a Civil Defence training centre. Since this organisation was disbanded in 1968, it has been used as an auction house, and is now a large antiques centre and café.

The viaduct was blown up in two stages during 1969, despite local residents' attempts to save it.

The ancient town of Battle has the next station up the line. Its station buildings were constructed in keeping with the abbey for which the town is famous. It once boasted a goods yard, but this is now covered by the station car park, with the present facilities being just an Up and Down platform.

Just outside Robertsbridge, gypsum was discovered in 1873 and three years later mining started. The mine had its own network of sidings, and rail was used to transport the majority of its output. The mine remains open, with freight trains still operating.

Robertsbridge was reached from Tunbridge Wells in September 1851 and was temporarily a terminus before the line was extended south. In 1900 it became the junction with the Rother Valley Light Railway, which was built by Colonel Stephens. It wound its way through the Sussex villages of Bodiam and Northiam before crossing the county border and passing through the picturesque town of Tenterden. In 1905 the line was extended to join the main line to Dover at Headcorn, and its name was changed to the Kent & East Sussex Railway. Passenger services were withdrawn in 1954 and the section between Tenterden and Headcorn closed completely. The line from Robertsbridge to Tenterden stayed open for freight until 1961. The Rother Valley Railway (East Sussex) Ltd was formed in 1991 and based at Robertsbridge. Their aim, with the approval of the K&ESR, was to reinstate the line from Robertsbridge to Bodiam. The idea was then for the latter to operate the whole of the line from Tenterden to Robertsbridge. Sharing

Robertsbridge with the rail network would increase patronage on the line, as it did when the Bluebell reached East Grinstead.

Etchingham station opened in 1851 with the opening of the railway. It is a simple two-road station. The main station building was partly built using sandstone blocks from a manor house that once stood on the site.

Stonegate is then reached. On opening in 1851 it was called Witherenden, but only kept this name for a matter of months before it became Ticehurst Road. It kept this name until 1947 when it became Stonegate. Old photographs show it only having one platform but there was a passing loop. A second platform was added, accessible via a footbridge.

Wadhurst is next up the line and, like other stations on the line, it was designed by William Tress and built in red brick, resembling a large house. It also had a goods yard and shed, with coal being delivered for local merchants. The signal box that was built there is now in use on the K&ESR at Northiam.

The local Sunday school used to organise an annual outing to Hastings for the children of the parish, who would have to wear coloured ribbons on the beach so that they could be identified. For a number of years this was run by Mrs Margaret Manktelow and after the war, the engine would carry a headboard declaring it 'Maggie's Special'.

Frant was the last station in Sussex before the border with Kent was crossed and Tunbridge Wells reached. It was also designed by William Tress, the company's

Wadhurst station, showing the staggered platforms. Other SER stations were built like this so that passengers could cross the line, even if both platforms were occupied. The footbridge was a later addition to the station. (The John Law Collection)

The Wealden Limited was run on 14 August 1955 with E1 No. 31019 and D No. 31737 in charge of this leg of the journey.

architect; he designed it in the Gothic style, using local ragstone. It has been a listed building since 1982.

The line from Tonbridge to Hastings cuts through the High Weald, and eight tunnels had to be bored. The cost of the railway from Tunbridge Wells to Hastings was £725,000, but it has been well documented that the builder of the line skimped on the brick lining of tunnels, with only four layers of bricks being used rather than the stipulated six. This came to light when, in March 1855, part of the brickwork inside Mountfield tunnel collapsed. Inspections of other tunnels on the route showed that three more, the Grove Hill, Strawberry Hill and Wells tunnels, all had insufficient layers of bricks, with Grove Hill having only one layer of bricks. Re-boring the tunnels would have proved to be too costly, so more layers were added to the existing brickwork, restricting the loading gauge through them. In 1862 Wadhurst tunnel too collapsed, also due to insufficient layers of bricks. This meant that all engines and rolling stock had to be built to a restricted loading gauge, so as to run safely down the line. This situation continued until the line was electrified in 1986 and the opportunity was taken to single the line through the tunnels.

Heading east from Hastings station is the line through Rye to Ashford. Ore is the first station that is encountered on the other side of the 230-yard Mount Pleasant tunnel. Building this tunnel created problems, as the soft earth that was removed to form the tunnel was piled up on the embankment. In 1860 there was a massive landslide and tons of earth blocked the tunnel entrance. The tunnel had to be lengthened and walls built to hold the earth back. This was as far as the 1930s electrification scheme reached. It opened in January 1888 to serve the expanding north-east area of Hastings. It had a goods yard

Hastings also had a steam miniature railway at the eastern end of the promenade. The railway still exists but it is no longer powered by steam.

and sidings that served the Hastings Tramways power station and, when that closed in 1925, the new Broomgrove power station. Later there used to be a servicing centre for electric units operating the coastal service to Brighton but, when the line to Tunbridge Wells was electrified, these facilities were transferred to St Leonards.

On the other side of Ore station is Ore tunnel, which measures 1,402 yards. Beyond that is Three Oaks. It opened as Three Oaks Bridge Halt in 1907 when the line was double track. In 1909 it became Three Oaks Halt before becoming Three Oaks and Guestling Halt, as it was decided that this station was closer to Guestling than Guestling Halt. The halt was dropped in 1969. There were also two other halts between Ore and Winchelsea. These were Snailham Crossing Halt and the original Guestling Halt.

Snailham opened in 1907 with platforms that could only accommodate a single coach, which was ample for the amount of patronage it had! It closed in 1959.

The original Guestling Halt was renamed 'Doleham Halt' when Three Oaks Halt became 'Three Oaks and Guestling Halt' with the Halt being dropped in 1969.

Winchelsea is one of the larger centres of population along the line but the station is over half a mile from the village along a narrow, unlit country lane. The station buildings have now become a private dwelling and the station is unstaffed.

The ancient port of Rye is the next station along the line. This is the line's largest station with two platforms either side of a passing loop. There was a branch to Rye Harbour, which branched off just to the west of Rye station. This carried on for about 1.5 miles to the south on the west side of the River Tillingham. It was built as a goods-only line in 1854 to serve various industries at the harbour and was lifted in 1962.

The diminutive 2-4-0 loco *Camber* poses with driver and station staff. I'm not sure engine drivers should wear white trousers – his didn't stay white for long! The other loco on the line was called *Victoria* and they were both built by Bagnalls of Stafford.

The SER line was not the only railway in Rye, however. There was a narrow-gauge railway called the Rye & Camber Tramway, built to a 3-foot gauge. 'Tramway' was a term used for a railway built entirely on private land that did not need an Act of Parliament to construct. If it had been built a year later, after the Light Railways Act had come into force, it would have been classed as one. It was built to transport golfers and holiday makers to golf links and the sea. Apart from Rye station, there were two others: Golf Links, a through station, and Camber, the terminus at the other end of the 1.75-mile-long track. It was designed by Holman Stephens, who was also responsible for the Rother Valley Railway, and opened in 1895 as far as Golf Links. Bathers had to wait another thirteen years before an extension was built to take them to the beach. Passenger services were stopped at the outbreak of the Second World War, but the line stayed open and a new siding was laid by Canadian troops as part of a plan to lay a pipeline under the Atlantic Ocean. Lack of maintenance during the war years took a terrible toll on the railway; it was deemed uneconomical to repair and was sold for scrap in 1947, with the Rye & Camber Tramway Company being wound up two years later. Golf Links station still survives and the track bed has been turned into a footpath.

Brighton Works and Shed

Most of the locomotives in the images in this book were built at the works in Brighton and were supplied for everyday working from the shed at Brighton or one of its sub sheds.

From the 1850s the workshops were built, adjacent to the station. Before the works were built at Brighton, the locomotives were maintained at New Cross Gate; however, space was at a premium there and new works were needed. J. Craven, who was the Chief Mechanical Engineer for the LB&SCR from 1847 to 1869, was responsible for the creation of the works in Brighton. The site of the works was on a steep hillside, and much of the workshops had to be supported by stilts. The original engine shed was also sited there, and this had to be moved to the land between the main line and west coast line. This presented its own difficulty because this area had been used to store a mountain of chalk excavated to create the flat surface needed to build the station. Moving this chalk took six or seven years. Much went to Kingston Wharf, where the docks were being expanded, and some was used to level the site to be used for the goods yard.

The first engines to emerge from the works were in 1852 and were two single-driver well tanks.

William Stroudley took over in 1870; it is said that at that time there were seventy-two different classes of locomotives. His policy was to rationalise these and produce six classes with interchangeable parts.

After Stroudley's death, he was succeeded in 1890 by R. J. Billinton, who continued to expand the works to meet the demands of the railway. It was he who expanded the works by using stilts to support the buildings. This extension was 430 feet long and tapered between 41 and 53 feet wide. This extension was built over the goods line. The extension allowed twelve new locos a year to be built, as well as the forty to fifty being repaired or maintained. By 1896, the LB&SCR's Locomotive Dept. employed 3,850 staff, of whom 2,200 were employed at Brighton.

More room for locomotive construction was obtained by moving the carriage works to Lancing, which was not fully operational until 1912.

Mr D. Earle Marsh succeeded R. Billinton in 1905. He created more space by adding a new storey over the Westinghouse shops. In 1908, the works were connected to the town's electricity supply and the steam-generated electricity plant was scrapped, except for within the paint shop.

1911 saw L. B. Billinnton (son of R. J.) take over as CME. Much of his time there was during the First World War, when the works were used for the production of munitions.

The last class of engine to be produced by the LB&SCR at the works were the 4-6-4 Class L tanks, which were later converted to N15X 4-6-0s. The last one was named *Remembrance* in honour of those workers who lost their lives in the First World War. It was introduced in April 1922. L. B. Billington was the last of the LB&SCR CMEs, as he stayed until the Southern Railway was created in 1923, which was when R. Maunsell was appointed.

The Southern Railway moved much of its locomotive construction to Ashford and Eastleigh, although Brighton continued to service locos.

Oliver Bulleid became the last CME in 1937 before the railways were nationalised in 1948, and he came up with a number of revolutionary new ideas. The Second World War saw Brighton used once again for locomotive building and it was re-equipped to build most of the 110 West Country/Battle of Britain Class, as well as the forty Q1s, with a total of 104 locomotives being built.

Originally LB&SCR Class A1 No. 35, *Morden* entered service in June 1878. It was placed on the duplicate list and renumbered 635 on November 1908. Rebuilt to A1X standard in April 1922, it became Southern Railway No. 2635 after 1923. It was then transferred to service stock, renumbered 377S, repainted black and lettered 'Loco.Dept.B'ton' in August 1946, replacing A1 class 380S, the former LB&SCR No. 82 *Boxhill* when that locomotive was withdrawn for preservation. Subsequently it was repainted Stroudley passenger-engine green and lettered 'BRIGHTON WORKS' during 1947. After Brighton Works closed, No. 377S returned to capital stock and was renumbered 32635, still retaining the Stroudley livery. Finally, it was wthdrawn in March 1963 and broken up at Eastleigh.

After nationalisation, the works continued to build new engines with the last one, No. 80154, being out-shopped in 1956.

Demolition of the site began in 1969 and it is now a car park.

The shed that was responsible for supplying steam engines for passenger and freight services in the area was built between the main line and the west coast lines. It measured 158 feet by 201 feet, with fourteen roads. This stood next to another three-road shed 483 feet long. This was known as 'new shed' and was used for preparing locos for their next tour of duty. Locos leaving the main shed had to do so via the station, as there was no exit to the north or east.

Electrification in the 1930s saw a decrease in the number of locos needed, but there were still secondary routes that relied on steam power. When these were closed in the 1960s there was no need for the shed and it closed. The site is now covered by an industrial estate.

Std 4 2-6-4T No. 80010 under construction in Brighton Works on 30 June 1951.

An unidentified A1X inside Brighton Works on an unknown date.

Bulleid's Leader being moved by works shunter AIX No. 377S. (Brian Matthews)

Class C2X No. 32541 at Brighton on 16 May 1951.

Brighton constructed some engines to LMS designs, and No. 42096 was one of these. It was a 2-6-4T and a forerunner to the BR Std 4 class, constructed at Brighton Works.

An overall view of the main shed at Brighton in BR days. On the right of the photograph is the large water tank and the water-softening plant, which was needed due to the calcium in the water from the chalky South Downs.

25 October 1952 saw Class C2X No. 32440 at its home shed of Brighton.

The fireman breaks up the larger lumps of coal on Schools Class No. 30928 *Stowe* at Brighton on 24 February 1962.